By Good and
Necessary
Consequence

Explorations in
Reformed Confessional Theology

Editors
Daniel R. Hyde and Mark Jones

By Good and Necessary Consequence

Ryan M. McGraw

REFORMATION HERITAGE BOOKS
Grand Rapids, Michigan

By Good and Necessary Consequence
© 2012 by Ryan M. McGraw

Reformation Heritage Books
2965 Leonard St. NE
Grand Rapids, MI 49525
616-977-0889 / Fax 616-285-3246
orders@heritagebooks.org
www.heritagebooks.org

Printed in the United States of America
12 13 14 15 16 17/10 9 8 7 6 5 4 3 2 1

Library of Congress Cataloging-in-Publication Data

McGraw, Ryan M.
  By good and necessary consequence / Ryan M. McGraw.
      p. cm. — (Explorations in Reformed confessional theology)
  Includes bibliographical references (p.   ) and index.
  ISBN 978-1-60178-182-6 (pbk. : alk. paper) 1. Theology, Doctrinal. 2. Bible—Hermeneutics. 3. Westminster Confession of Faith. I. Title.
  BT75.3.M36 2012
  230'.42—dc23

                            2012011262

For additional Reformed literature, request a free book list from Reformation Heritage Books at the above address.

To Dr. Joseph A. Pipa

*father, mentor, professor,
counselor, and friend*

Contents

Series Preface

The creeds of the ancient church and the doctrinal standards of the sixteenth- and seventeenth-century Reformed churches are rich theological documents. They summarize the essential teachings of Scripture, express biblical doctrines in meaningful and memorable ways, and offer pastoral guidance for the heads and hearts of God's people. Nevertheless, when twenty-first-century readers pick up these documents, certain points may be found confusing, misunderstood, or irrelevant for the church.

The Exploration in Reformed Confessional Theology series intends to clarify some of these confessional issues from four vantage points. First, it views confessional issues from the *textual* vantage point, exploring such things as variants, textual development, and the development of language within the documents themselves as well as within the context in which these documents were written. Second, this series views confessional issues from the *historical* vantage point, exploring social history and the history of ideas that shed light upon these issues. Third, this series views confessional issues from the *theological* vantage point, exploring the issues of intra- and interconfessional theology both in the days these documents were written as well as our day. Fourth, this series views confessional issues from the *pastoral* vantage point, exploring the pressing pastoral needs of certain doctrines and the implications of any issues that cause difficulty in the confessions.

In exploring our vast and deep heritage in such a way, our ultimate goal is to "walk worthy of the Lord unto all pleasing, being fruitful in every good work, and increasing in the knowledge of God" (Col. 1:10).

—Daniel R. Hyde and Mark Jones

Author's Preface

Some have noted that systematic theology has fallen on hard times.[1] Systematic theology is often contrasted with or set in opposition to biblical theology and to exegesis. Some accuse systematics of presupposing a theological grid that imposes itself on the text of Scripture, thus twisting the Scriptures and relying upon "proof texts" that have been violently wrested out of their proper context. What does that have to do with this little book on the principle of "good and necessary consequence" in a series titled Explorations in Reformed Confessional Theology? A close relationship exists between the widespread distrust of systematic theology and the neglect or denial of the statement found in Westminster Confession of Faith (WCF) 1:6: "The whole counsel of God concerning all things necessary for His own glory, man's salvation, faith and life, is either expressly set down in Scripture, *or by good*

---

1. For a treatment of contemporary criticisms of theology, see J. I. Packer, "Is Systematic Theology a Mirage? An Introductory Discussion," in *Doing Theology in Today's World: Essays in Honor of Kenneth S. Kantzer*, ed. John D. Woodbridge and Thomas Edward McKomisky (Grand Rapids: Zondervan, 1991), 17–37.

and necessary consequence may be deduced from Scripture" (emphasis added). Exegesis and biblical theology tell us what the words of Scripture mean or what distinguishes a particular biblical author from others, yet both often stop short of drawing theological conclusions from Scripture that show us what the Bible teaches as a whole. This is the task of systematic theology, which depends heavily on deducing divinely intended consequences from the text of Scripture. Without such deductions and the conclusions that are based upon them, we lose the ability to ask important questions of the Bible, such as what it teaches about the relationship between the persons of the Holy Trinity.[2]

For this reason, I was enthusiastic when Reformation Heritage Books asked me to expand the first chapter of my ThM thesis from Greenville Presbyterian Theological Seminary into a small book.[3] I have long believed that this subject is more important to the life and theology of

---

2. An illuminating example of this is found in Andreas Kostenberger's treatment of the Trinity in his work on the theology of John's gospel and letters. He presents the biblical data concerning the unity of the Godhead and addresses relevant passages in John relating to each of the three persons. Yet without drawing inferences from and systematizing the biblical data that he has collected, major questions such as whether each person possesses a distinct personality and whether the persons of the Godhead are subordinated to one another remain unanswered. Andreas J. Kostenberger, *A Theology of John's Gospel and Letters* (Grand Rapids: Zondervan, 2009), 355–402.

3. Ryan McGraw, "The Consequences of Reformed Worship: The Call to Worship, Baptism, the Offering, and the Benediction in Corporate Worship" (ThM thesis, Greenville Presbyterian Theological Seminary, 2008).

the church than many people realize. In this principle, as the Westminster Assembly of Divines stated it, lies not only a crucial justification of the importance and method of systematic theology, but also a key to understanding New Testament uses of the Old Testament, a solid connection between exposition and application in preaching, personal assurance of salvation, and the manner in which Jesus Himself interpreted the Scriptures.

In accord with the purpose of the Explorations in Reformed Confessional Theology series, I have sought to address "textual, historical, theological, and pastoral issues" as well as matters of contemporary significance in connection to Westminster Confession of Faith 1.6. However, I have inverted this order slightly by beginning with the biblical foundations of the principle of "good and necessary consequence," followed by a section that addresses the principle in its historical context. I have done this largely because many readers may immediately recoil from the idea that anything other than what is "expressly set down in Scripture" is a proper means of discerning "the whole counsel of God." Such readers will not likely be interested in how the Westminster divines understood and used the principle until they are convinced that such a principle is demanded by Scripture. Therefore, I begin in chapter 1 with a short definition and illustration of the principle, followed by the relevant scriptural data, relying heavily upon the indispensable necessity of the principle from the teaching of the Lord Jesus Christ. Next, in chapter 2, I draw attention to textual and historical issues, including the use of the principle by contemporaries of the Westminster Confession of Faith and the Westminster Catechisms. On the heels of this discussion, I treat the need for "necessary consequence" in four major areas of theology in chapter 3. Given the many objections to this principle, I address some of the more significant ones in chapter 4. Finally, in chapter 5 I draw some practical conclusions that affect the life of the Reformed church in relation to her confession of faith, her Bible reading, and her preaching.

I would like to thank Jay Collier for suggesting that I write this book, and Danny Hyde for officially inviting me to do so. Mark Jones deserves hearty thanks as well, not only for his labors on this series but also for going above and beyond the call of duty as a mentor for my PhD project at the same time. I cannot adequately express the thanks that Dr. Jones deserves as a diligent servant of the Lord. This work would not have been possible without the help and encouragement of Dr. Joseph A. Pipa, who supervised my ThM thesis. My mother-in-law, Sylvia Stevens, read the entire manuscript as well and made indispensable stylistic suggestions. I am grateful to Brian Pendelton for helping me to complete some final references. My wife, Krista, always encourages me to stay on top of my many projects, especially when I am overwhelmed and discouraged. Her help has been a great comfort to my soul. Lastly and most importantly, I bless the triune God for counting me faithful and putting me into the ministry, as well as for giving me opportunities to be useful in His kingdom.

1

Biblical Foundations

Like the church at Berea, all godly Christians desire to test what they read and hear by the Word of God. This is an indispensable necessity for our Christian growth, for our maturity in the faith, and for guarding against error. We should call no man father or teacher, since our Father is in heaven and Christ is our true Teacher (Matt. 23:8–10). When believers in the Lord Jesus hear teachings and doctrines unfamiliar to them, they demand, properly, "Show me in the Bible!" Yet a biblical answer to this mandate will not always come by citing chapter and verse. There are some doctrines (such as the doctrine of the Trinity) that are dear to Christians, but that cannot be proved by any single passage of Scripture. Such doctrines must be inferred and pieced together from several passages of Scripture. For this reason the Westminster Confession of Faith asserts, "The whole counsel of God concerning all things necessary for His own glory, man's salvation, faith and life, is either expressly set down in Scripture, or by *good and necessary consequence may be deduced from Scripture*: unto which nothing at any time is to be added, whether new revelations of the Spirit or traditions of men" (1.6, emphasis added).

Many have accused this principle of "good and necessary consequence" set forth in the Westminster Confession of Faith of being esoteric, taking the Bible out of the hands of the average believer, and doing violence to the Scriptures. However, the teaching and example of the Bible itself necessitates this principle: it has been recognized as indispensable in the theology of the church, and it is biblically sound in spite of the various objections leveled against it. Without the appropriate use of good and necessary consequence, it is impossible to establish vital biblical doctrines, to apply the Reformed or regulative principle of worship to the extent intended by God, to discern some necessary applications that flow from biblical teachings, and to understand the manner in which the New Testament authors used the Old Testament. While it would make sense to delve into the history of this principle in the context of the Westminster Assembly first, I have chosen to delay a full discussion of the historical background until the next chapter in order to convince the reader that this subject is of interest primarily because it is rooted in Scripture. For these reasons, it is vital to establish the principle of good and necessary consequence from Scripture first and then to proceed to the historical setting of the Westminster Confession of Faith.[1]

---

1. In addition to the sources that I have cited below, two recent articles explain and defend the use of good and necessary consequences. See C. J. Williams, "Good and Necessary Consequence in the

Defining the Phrase

A definition of good and necessary consequence is already implicit in the first chapter of the Westminster Confession of Faith. Good and necessary consequence is distinguished from matters concerning God's glory, man's salvation, and faith or life that are "expressly set down in Scripture." This includes direct precepts, prohibitions, statements of truth, and clearly approved examples. According to this statement, the term "good and necessary consequence" refers to doctrines and precepts that are truly contained in and intended by the divine Author of Scripture, yet are not found or stated on the surface of the text and must be legitimately inferred from one or more passages of Scripture. As the phrase indicates, such inferences must be "good," or legitimately drawn from the text of Scripture. In addition, they must be "necessary," as opposed to imposed or arbitrary.[2]

Westminster Confession," in *The Faith Once Delivered: Essays in Honor of Wayne R. Spear*, ed. Anthony T. Selvaggio (Phillipsburg, N.J.: P&R, 2007), 171–190; and Richard A. Muller and Rowland S. Ward, *Scripture and Worship: Biblical Interpretation and the Directory for Worship* (Phillipsburg, N.J.: P&R, 2007), 59–82. The former article defends the principle from Scripture in brief and provides valuable illustrative material from George Gillespie. The value of the latter article is that it demonstrates in detail the manner in which the Westminster divines themselves used the principle in their annotations on Scripture. This latter point is addressed in the following chapter.

2. Louis Berkhof, *Principles of Biblical Interpretation* (Grand Rapids: Baker, 1950), 159–60. This is one of the few relatively contemporary manuals on biblical interpretation that includes a section on the "theological" reading of Scripture.

The nineteenth-century Scottish Presbyterian James Bannerman (1807–1868) has provided a useful illustration of what this principle entails in practice. Genesis 1:1 states, "In the beginning God created the heaven and the earth." The inferences that may (and must) be drawn from this passage are: (1) that God and nature are distinct (as opposed to pantheism); (2) that matter had a beginning and that only God is eternal (as opposed to various forms of materialism); and (3) that God created matter out of nothing without using any preexisting materials (as opposed to various theories of emanation).[3]

To ensure that the conclusions obtained by use of this principle are truly biblical, the premises must be biblically certain. In the first part of the example given from Genesis 1:1, it is certain that God is the Creator of heaven and earth. Nature is included in the "heaven and the earth" that God made. Therefore, it is a necessary (and clear) conclusion that God and nature are distinct. Additionally, the proper way to use inferences from Scripture can be clarified by illustrating their abuse. For example, in the book of Joshua, God commanded the sun to "stand still" in the sky. During the time of the Reformation, men such as Martin Luther insisted this proved that the sun revolved around

---

3. James Bannerman, *The Church of Christ: A Treatise on the Nature, Power, Ordinances, Discipline, and Government of the Christian Church* (1868; repr., Birmingham, Ala.: Solid Ground Christian Books, 2009), 2:410. I have prepared an abridgement, outline, and study guide for Bannerman's magisterial work on ecclesiology, which is forthcoming through Solid Ground Christian Books.

the earth and not vice versa. They declared any other theory to be contrary to Scripture. Yet the text simply describes the sun from man's earthbound perspective, just as today people still speak of the sun "moving" across the sky or "rising" and "setting." Even with knowledge of modern science, we do not speak of an "earthrise" or "earthset" because these terms do not accurately describe our visual perspective. The Bible neither denies nor requires that the sun revolve around the earth—it bypasses the question. The only sort of necessary conclusions that can be derived from this passage is that God is sovereign over the natural progression of day and night and that He is able to alter its course whenever and however He pleases. Moreover, the principle of good and necessary consequence is not a license to allegorize our interpretations of Scripture or to impose the ideas of men upon the Word of God.[4] Rather, its purpose is to recognize unavoidable implications from the text of Scripture. These inferences ordinarily reflect the theological framework that the texts of the Bible assume and merely reveal these underlying assumptions by making them explicit.

---

4. One of the most illuminating treatments of how the Reformed tradition developed careful rules of biblical interpretation in order to avoid allegory is found in Henry Knapp, "Understanding the Mind of God: John Owen and Seventeenth-Century Exegetical Methodology" (PhD diss., Calvin Theological Seminary, 2002), 282–93.

How Jesus Used This Principle

The question of primary importance is whether or not the Bible permits the church to use good and necessary consequence, and whether the Scriptures are sufficiently clear with respect to this matter. The biblical authors used the principle of good and necessary consequence, particularly in New Testament citations of the Old Testament.[5] This is most notable in the practice of the Lord Jesus Christ Himself, but it is prevalent in the writings of the apostles as well. The following examples demonstrate that this hermeneutical principle is not only permissible, but that it is mandated.

Matthew 22:29–32

The most commonly treated example of good and necessary consequence is Jesus' reply to the Sadducees concerning the truth of the resurrection of the dead as recorded in Matthew 22:29–32.[6] In the beginning of the chapter, the Lord Jesus Christ told a parable that condemned the

---

5. I will explore this point in more detail below. The same observations are in order with respect to how the Old Testament authors used earlier portions of the Old Testament, but as O. Palmer Robertson observes, very little study has been devoted to this question. See O. Palmer Robertson, *Prophet of the Coming Day of the Lord: The Message of Joel* (Durham, UK: Evangelical Press, 1995), 12.

6. Virtually all defenses that I have found of "good and necessary consequence" begin with a discussion of this passage. For examples, see Berkhof, *Principles of Biblical Interpretation*, 159; Bannerman, *Church of Christ*, 412; Francis Turretin, *Institutes of Elenctic Theology*, ed. James Dennison Jr., trans. George Musgrave Giger (Phillipsburg: P&R, 1992), 1:39; Benjamin Breckinridge Warfield, "The Westminster

Pharisees by likening them to the invited guests of a wedding feast who, when the time came to attend the feast, rudely rejected the invitation. As a result, the master of the feast invited strangers in their place. By this parable, Jesus condemned the Pharisees, who ought to have welcomed Him with joy as their long-awaited Messiah. Consequently, the offended Pharisees "went…and took counsel how they might entangle him in his talk" (Matt. 22:15). However, the Lord Jesus, who is the only wise God and in whom are hidden all the treasures of wisdom and knowledge (Col. 2:3), soundly refuted their assault in such a manner that even his enemies "marveled" at his answer (Matt. 22:22). The Sadducees, who said that "there is no resurrection, neither angel, nor spirit" (Acts 23:8), immediately seized the opportunity to do better than their rivals and posed a question to Jesus that they believed to be unanswerable. In the guise of asking Jesus an honest question, they began by citing the biblical principle that when a man died his brother had the duty to marry his widow and beget children on behalf of his brother (Deut. 25:5). After presenting a scenario in which seven brothers all died successively after marrying the same woman, they asked, "Therefore in the resurrection whose wife shall she be of the seven? For they all had her" (Matt. 22:28). In their minds, this scenario created an insurmountable problem, making the resurrection of the dead a logical absurdity. Since it was

Doctrine of Holy Scripture," in *The Works of B. B. Warfield* (1932; repr., Grand Rapids: Baker, 2003), 6:224–26.

unthinkable that a woman should have seven husbands in this life or in the life to come, and because each husband died having the right to call her his wife, then the resurrection of the dead must be a farce.[7]

In reply, Jesus asserted that the Sadducees were in error at two points: "Ye do err [lit., are "deceived" or "led astray"], *not knowing the scriptures*, nor the power of God" (v. 29, emphasis added). The accusation that they were ignorant of the Scriptures is particularly relevant when considering the question of good and necessary consequence. Jesus noted that the Sadducees had excluded a vital option from their reasoning: "But they which shall be accounted worthy to obtain that world, and the resurrection from the dead, neither marry, nor are given in marriage" (Luke 20:35).[8] He proceeded to demonstrate that the resurrection was clearly and convincingly taught in the Scriptures. Those who are familiar with the Old Testament may express surprise that Jesus did not attempt to prove the resurrection from one of the nearly

---

7. Ironically, the Sadducees assumed the principle of good and necessary consequence in this line of argumentation. Jesus' answer simultaneously illustrates both the improper use of this principle by the Sadducees and its proper use by Jesus Himself.

8. "The resurrection life in which the Sadducees did not believe was being conceived of as marked by strong continuity with the arrangements of the life of the present. However, the view of the resurrection life that is rejected by the Sadducees as *more* than possible (thus the conundrum) is to be rejected by Jesus as *less* than is to be anticipated." John Nolland, *The Gospel of Matthew: A Commentary on the Greek Text* (Grand Rapids: Eerdmans, 2005), 904.

express statements contained in such passages as Psalm 16, Isaiah 26, or from a few relevant texts in Job. Instead, Christ chose to cite the Exodus passage about the burning bush (Mark 12:26; Ex. 3:6, 15), in which God said, "I am the God of Abraham, the God of Isaac, and the God of Jacob."[9] Jesus concluded, "God is not the God of the dead, but of the living" (Matt. 22:32).

It is vital for us to grasp the import of Jesus' line of argumentation in this passage. Jesus did not respond with a simple and direct proof text for the doctrine of the resurrection. Instead, He drew a conclusion from a well-known passage, which Bannerman described as "an inference the force of which it may be fairly said to require a certain amount of thought and spiritual insight to fully perceive."[10] Jesus rested His argument primarily on the fact that God had said "*I am* the God of Abraham," etc., as opposed to "*I was*." If God was currently the God of the patriarchs when He spoke to Moses, and if "God is not the God of the dead but of the living," then the patriarchs must still have been alive at that time (which the Sadducees denied), even though they had died physically.

However, modern readers will likely sense that there is a missing piece in the argument. The continuing existence of Abraham, Isaac, and Jacob certainly proves the immortality of the *soul*, but how is this relevant to the

---

9. It is probable that Jesus chose to answer with a passage from the Pentateuch because that was the only part of the Old Testament that the Sadducees held to be authoritative.

10. Bannerman, *Church of Christ*, 2:412.

resurrection of the *body*, which was the central focus of this debate? As William Hendriksen correctly reminds us, "The men with whom this immutable Jehovah established an everlasting covenant were Israelites, not Greeks."[11] In contrast to the Greeks, who viewed the body as the "prison-house" of the soul from which the soul sought liberation, the Jewish people conceived of man as a unit consisting of body and soul. For this reason, redemption must take place in both body and soul, if it is to take place at all. The New Testament reflects the importance of the body by referring to the physical bodies of believers as being the temple of the Holy Spirit of God. Redeemed man was purchased both body and soul with the precious blood of the Lord Jesus Christ. For this reason, man is obligated to serve God with his body as well as his spirit, since both are the Lord's (1 Cor. 6:19–20). In 1 Corinthians 15, the apostle Paul made the striking assertion that if there were no resurrection of the body (and consequently no resurrection of Christ), then those who had already died in Christ would have perished, thus extinguishing the entire substance of the Christian's hope (1 Cor. 15:18–19).[12] In this lengthy

---

11. William Hendriksen, *New Testament Commentary: Exposition of the Gospel according to Matthew* (Grand Rapids: Baker, 1973), 807.

12. For a study on the centrality of the resurrection in Paul's soteriology, see Richard B. Gaffin, *Resurrection and Redemption: A Study in Paul's Soteriology* (Phillipsburg, N.J.: P&R, 1987). See also the comments in Anthony C. Thiselton, *The First Epistle to the Corinthians, New International Greek Testament Commentary* (Grand Rapids: Eerdmans, 2000), 1214–22.

discussion of the resurrection, Paul's underlying assumption was that unless man is redeemed in both body and soul, then he is not redeemed at all. This same assumption underlies Jesus' response to the Sadducees.

The remarkable thing about this passage of Scripture is that by a single argument, Jesus "had put the Sadducees to silence" (Matt. 22:34). In other words, they capitulated under the weight of the Lord's indomitable argument, and they tacitly conceded His point. When the crowd of spectators heard these things, they also "were astonished at his doctrine" (v. 33). Part of the shame of the Sadducees may have been that, although this was such a well-known passage of Scripture, the implicit doctrine of the resurrection contained in it had consistently slipped under their noses. It is important that Jesus refuted His opponents *by their own admission* without demonstrating that the resurrection was "expressly set down in Scripture." The resurrection of the dead was not directly in view in the context in which the burning bush passage appears in this dialogue. Instead, Jesus' argument was deduced and, by good and necessary consequence, drawn from the text. The conclusions that He inferred from the passage were both "good" and "necessary." Some might object that since Christ and His apostles were infallible, they came to their conclusions solely by divine inspiration, and therefore we cannot imitate them in their use of the Old Testament Scriptures in this manner. Yet, as Francis Turretin (1623–1687) observed, the Sadducees did not acknowledge Jesus' authority; it was

His reasoning alone that stopped their mouths.[13] Far from twisting the Scriptures by insisting that there are things necessary for faith, life, salvation, and the glory of God that are not "expressly set down in Scripture" but that are drawn from it by good and necessary consequence, Christ demonstrated that *by failing to do this*, the Sadducees were ignorant of the teaching of Scripture (v. 29). He asked them sarcastically, "Have ye *not read* that which was spoken unto you by God?" (v. 31). Let us take heed not only of Jesus' example but also of His expectations!

Luke 24:25–27 and Other Passages

The example set forth in Matthew 22:29–32 is so decisive that even if it is considered in isolation, it establishes the legitimate use of good and necessary consequence. Yet it is far from being an isolated example. The assumption of this principle by the Lord echoes His expectation in Luke 24:25–27 that His disciples ought to have understood all

---

13. Turretin, *Institutes*, 1:39. In the nineteenth century, Patrick Fairbairn (1805–1874) noted that several German scholars had criticized Jesus' use of this text to prove the resurrection as an example of first-century "Rabbinic hairsplitting" and "cabalistic exposition." Aside from the irreverence involved in such an accusation, Fairbairn noted the similarity of such critics to Jesus' original audience: "Most worthy successors truly to those Saducean objectors whom our Lord sought to confute—equally shallow in their notions of God, and equally at fault in their reading of his written word!" Patrick Fairbairn, *Typology of Scripture* (1900; repr., Grand Rapids: Kregel, 1989), 1:366. However, the one advantage the Sadducees had over those who have adopted their critical spirit in modern times is that they at least were able to see the force of our Lord's argument.

that Moses and the prophets had spoken concerning the sufferings of the Christ and the glories that should follow. The name of Jesus is never explicitly named in the Law and the Prophets, yet Jesus expected His disciples to be able to identify Him as the suffering Christ in every part of the Old Testament.[14]

Nearly every New Testament citation of the Old Testament is an application of the principle of good and necessary consequence. When the faith of John the Baptist faltered, Jesus merely pointed to His miraculous deeds and to His preaching. He encouraged John by implying that the Old Testament prophecies were being fulfilled in Him and that no other could be the Messiah. In his Pentecost sermon, Peter asserted the necessity of Christ's resurrection as an inference drawn from the fact that not every part of Psalm 16 was applicable to David, since his tomb still remained with them. Peter grounded his line of argumentation, in great detail, on the fact that his assertion was not visible on the surface of the text (Acts 2:25– 31). In the first chapter of Hebrews, the author strung together an intricate chain of implications from several Old Testament passages, proving that the Son is both greater than the angels and that He is the God whose throne is forever and ever. By assuming that Psalm 102

---

14. Turretin, *Institutes*, 1:39. Incidentally, this demonstrates that even true disciples of the Lord who love Him and whom He loves do not understand many things in the Scriptures. Yet it is humbling to bear in mind that this warranted the statement of Christ that they were foolish and slow of heart (Luke 24:25).

referred to the Messiah rather than God the Father, the author next inferred that it was Jesus who laid the foundation of the earth (Heb. 1:10–12).[15] In Matthew 2:23, the apostle stated, "And he came and dwelt in a city called Nazareth: that it might be fulfilled which was spoken by the prophets, He shall be called a Nazarene." However, there is no prophecy in the Old Testament that explicitly mentions that the Christ would be called a Nazarene. Matthew appears to have deduced this from the overall testimony of the prophets.[16]

Good and necessary consequence is used by the authors of Scripture on a much larger scale than that of messianic prophecy. Since Psalm 109:8 petitions that the wicked

---

15. The book of Hebrews itself could be used as a case study in the use of Scripture consequences, since they are used so freely and often. Cf. Bannerman, *Church of Christ*, 2:413. For an older, but valuable, treatment of the use of the Old Testament in the book of Hebrews that is sensitive to good and necessary consequence, see B. F. Westcott, "On the Use of the O.T. in the Epistle," in *The Epistle to the Hebrews: The Greek Text with Notes and Essays* (1892; repr., Grand Rapids: Eerdmans, 1977), 469–95. Westcott states, "A study of the quotations from the O.T. in the Epistle brings light upon the whole relations of the Old Testament in the New, and upon the manner of the divine education of the world" (469).

16. It is possible that this text is designed to be a vague reference to Isaiah 9:1, in which the Messiah was said to bring light first to the land of Zebulun and Naphtali, since they were the first to have suffered from the captivity. Yet even if this is the case, Nazareth is not mentioned by name, but only the region in which Nazareth was found. See the insightful article by John Murray, "The Unity of the Old and New Testaments," in *The Collected Writings of John Murray* (Edinburgh: Banner of Truth, 1976), 23–26.

man should be cursed and be put to shame by means of another man filling his office, the apostles concluded that they ought to find a replacement for Judas in order to complete the number of the apostles prior to the outpouring of the Holy Spirit at Pentecost (Acts 1:20–22). In order to prove that ministers of the gospel have the right to be paid for their labors, the apostle Paul cited Deuteronomy 25:4: "Thou shalt not muzzle the ox when he treadeth out the corn." He extrapolated a broad principle from this text that had no direct relation to oxen, yet was legitimately derived from the passage. He asked his readers this: "Doth God take care for oxen? [i.e., "Is it oxen that God is concerned about here?"] Or saith he it altogether for our sakes?" (1 Cor. 9:9–10). He replied, "For our sakes, no doubt." Paul boldly asserted that the good and necessary consequence of this passage actually constituted the primary point of relevance to the New Testament church. According to the apostle, the principle lying behind this passage (to borrow the words of Jesus) is that "the labourer is worthy of his hire" (Luke 10:7). This is equally applicable to a man as it is to an ox. In Paul's estimation, limiting the meaning of this passage to that which is "expressly set down" in it is to miss the primary lesson of the passage.[17] This conclusion is neither an arbitrary nor an allegorical use of the text.

---

17. Partly for this reason, the Dutch *Nadere Reformatie* theologian Wilhelmus à Brakel (1635–1711) warned his readers from being overly dependent upon the context of Scripture. See Wilhelmus à Brakel, *The Christian's Reasonable Service*, ed. Joel R. Beeke, trans. Bartel Elshout (Grand Rapids: Reformation Heritage Books, 1992), 1:80.

Rather, it is a means of identifying the broad principles that underlie the passage in a manner that is comparable to the examples cited from Genesis 1:1.

Conclusion

If we could personally ask Christ and His apostles to prove various doctrines from the Scriptures, we might be surprised by some of the answers that we would receive. Christ and His apostles did not always support biblical doctrines by express statements derived from grammatical historical exegesis. They often established them by implications and deductions. B. B. Warfield summarized the significance of the example of the New Testament authors by stating that "the sense of Scripture is Scripture, and that men are bound by its whole sense in all its implications."[18] The examples provided illustrate that implications properly drawn from Scripture do not do violence to—but rather enlighten—the true meaning of Scripture as long as the inferences are clearly and legitimately drawn from the passages concerned. We do not have the excuse of claiming that only Christ and His apostles were able to interpret Scripture in this manner, since they expected both their followers and their opponents to be able to do so as well. It is a strong indictment against the church if Christ's enemies accept His methods of biblical interpretation more readily than His followers often do.

---

18. Warfield, "Westminster Doctrine of Scripture," 226.

2

The Westminster Assembly

The purpose of the Explorations in Reformed Confessional Theology series is to treat various aspects of the Reformed confession in light of history, Scripture, and contemporary relevance. "Good and necessary consequence" was codified as a principle in the first chapter of the Westminster Confession of Faith.[1] For this reason, it is important to set forth briefly the manner in which the Westminster divines and their contemporaries both formulated and used this principle in the context of the Westminster Assembly.

The Historical Context of Good and Necessary Consequence and the Westminster Assembly

The Westminster Assembly consisted largely of English ministers who were called by an English parliament to

---

1. The Westminster Confession of Faith (WCF) is more explicit than other preceding Reformed confessions on this point, including the Irish Articles (1615) and the Thirty-Nine Articles (1571) of the Church of England, both of which Westminster heavily relied upon. The addition is more of a clarification and expansion than an amendment.

establish English doctrine and church polity for English churches in the midst of the English Civil War.[2] Nevertheless, the Westminster Standards continue to serve as "the Presbyterian Standards"[3] in England, Scotland, America, and among other Presbyterian bodies throughout the world. This makes the Westminster Standards both a historical and a contemporary set of documents with continuing relevance. In spite of their decisively English context, the Westminster divines frequently interacted with theologians and churches in the rest of the Reformed world, and they desired to write a confession of faith and catechisms that would place them in line with Reformed orthodoxy generally.[4] Their statement on good

---

2. For the importance of the English context of the Westminster Assembly, see Robert Letham, *The Westminster Assembly: Reading Its Theology in Historical Context* (Phillipsburg, N.J.: P&R, 2009), 47–61. Letham's book presents a readable and balanced history of the Assembly that has corrected several earlier studies, most of which have placed too much emphasis upon the influence of the Scottish commissioners to the Assembly and have focused their attention on debates concerning church government, thus neglecting the theology of the Westminster divines as a whole.

3. This phrase is taken from Francis R. Beattie, *The Presbyterian Standards: An Exposition of the Westminster Confession of Faith and Catechisms* (Richmond, Va.: Southern Presbyterian Press, 1896).

4. Letham, *Westminster Assembly*, 84–98. For the international context, see Menna Prestwick, ed., *International Calvinism, 1541–1715* (Oxford: Clarendon Press, 1985); Willem van Asselt and Eef Dekker, eds., *Reformation and Scholasticism: An Ecumenical Enterprise* (Grand Rapids: Baker, 2001); Patrick Collinson, "England and International Calvinism, 1558–1640," in *From Cranmer to Sancroft* (New York: Hambledon Continuum, 2006), 75–100; Anthony

and necessary consequence in Westminster Confession of Faith 1.6 has respect to biblical interpretation (hermeneutics). In this respect, the international historical setting of Reformed orthodoxy is of equal importance with the English context. We will look briefly at the background of medieval hermeneutics together with its Reformed modifications, illustrate good and necessary consequence through the treatment of the principle by Scottish commissioner George Gillespie, and set forth some examples of the principle in seventeenth-century biblical interpretation through David Dickson's exposition of the Psalms.

The Medieval Background
Protestantism sought to modify some aspects of the medieval doctrine of Scripture and its interpretation.[5]

Milton, "Puritanism and the Continental Reformed Churches," in *The Cambridge Companion to Puritanism*, ed. John Coffey and Paul C. H. Lim (Cambridge: Cambridge University Press, 2008), 109–26. For a uniquely definitive treatment of the spread and development of Reformed churches internationally during the Reformation and Post-Reformation periods, see Philip Dixon, *Christ's Churches Purely Reformed: A Social History of Calvinism* (New Haven: Yale University Press, 2002).

5. For the sake of brevity, the following discussion is primarily adapted from Richard A. Muller, *Post-Reformation Reformed Dogmatics*, vol. 2, *Holy Scripture, The Cognitive Foundation of Theology* (Grand Rapids: Eerdmans, 2003). For more information on biblical interpretation among both medieval and Reformed interpreters, see Richard A. Muller and John L. Thompson, eds., *Biblical Interpretation in the Era of Reformation* (Grand Rapids: Eerdmans, 1996); and Donald K. McKim, ed., *Historical Handbook of Biblical Interpreters* (Westmont, Ill.: InterVarsity, 1998). For a useful popular treatment of the Protestant

From the time of Origen (185–254), the church had largely adopted what was referred to as the *quadriga* in biblical interpretation. This view asserted that there is a fourfold sense or meaning of any given text of Scripture. The historical sense (*historia*) regards the intent of the author in the original context. The allegorical sense (*allegoria*) is a spiritualized meaning of the text through the use of allegory, usually connected to Christ and the church. The tropological sense (*tropologia*) draws a moral or ethical meaning from the text. Lastly, the anagogical sense (*anagoge*) interprets the text in relation to heavenly things.[6] The Westminster Confession of Faith, by contrast, is representative of the Protestant rejection of this method when it states that "the true and full sense of Scripture…is not manifold, but one" (1.9). The "true and full sense of Scripture" might include compound elements such as an Old Testament type together with its New Testament antitype (as with John's interpretation of Moses lifting up the serpent in the wilderness in John 3:14). The Reformers viewed this imposition of a fourfold sense of biblical passages as both arbitrary and detrimental to the true meaning of the text.

However, in the later Middle Ages, some expositors, such as Hugh of St. Victor (d. 1141), Thomas Aquinas (d. 1274), and Albert the Great (d. 1280), gave priority to the historical or "literal" sense of Scripture. In their view,

---

doctrine of Scripture and its interpretation, see Keith A. Matthison, *The Shape of Sola Scriptura* (Moscow, Idaho: Canon Press, 2001).

6. Muller, *Post-Reformation Reformed Dogmatics*, 2:35.

the other three senses of the *quadriga* were valid and useful, but they must be rooted in the "literal" sense of the text. Aquinas even argued that the other three senses of the *quadriga* were not necessary for faith and practice.[7] The allegorical, tropological, and anagogical senses were primarily useful in the application of Scripture. These men also believed that the Scriptures were the ultimate and exclusive authority in matters of doctrine and practice, as opposed to those who believed that authority rested upon a combination of the Scriptures and the tradition of the church.[8] Medieval theologians added that some doctrinal conclusions (such as the Trinity) were not expressly set forth in Scripture, but must be deduced as necessary conclusions from various texts of Scripture. The church had defined and accepted many of these truths through councils and creeds.[9] Both of these themes became important in Protestant hermeneutics.

---

7. Muller, *Post-Reformation Reformed Dogmatics*, 2:36–37. For alternate medieval views on authority, see Heiko A. Oberman, *The Harvest of Medieval Theology: Gabriel Biel and Late Medieval Nominalism* (Grand Rapids: Baker, 2000), 361–422.

8. Muller, *Post-Reformation Reformed Dogmatics*, 2:51. Muller adds that in this period the theologians tended to place Scripture first, while the canon lawyers argued for a two-source theory composed of Scripture and tradition. The latter officially became the Roman Catholic view as codified in the Council of Trent. "Canones et Decreta Dogmatica Concilii Tridentini," 4th session, in *The Creeds of Christendom: With a History and Critical Notes*, ed. Philip Schaff (1931; repr., Grand Rapids: Baker, 1998), 2:80.

9. Muller, *Post-Reformation Reformed Dogmatics*, 2:54.

One of the problems faced by biblical interpreters in the Middle Ages (as well as by later Reformed theologians) related to the christological reading of the Old Testament.[10] Because the New Testament authors often asserted that Christ is the center of the Old Testament Scriptures (e.g. Luke 24:25–27, 44–45) and because they often applied various passages of the Old Testament to Him in a typological fashion, biblical expositors struggled to understand Old Testament texts in their historical contexts while simultaneously doing justice to the overarching christological scope of Scripture. In part, the *quadriga* represented an attempt to harmonize such difficulties. The Renaissance accentuated this difficulty with its emphasis upon the exposition of the Scriptures in the original languages, largely bypassing the theological analysis of texts that was prevalent in the Middle Ages.[11] This created a potential crisis for theology, since it tended to separate (or exclude) theology from the task of exegesis. While we may view the Protestant rejection of the *quadriga* as a welcome change following the Reformation, we should at least sympathize with the fact that medieval theologians were wrestling seriously with how our understanding of the New Testament should influence our exegesis of the Old Testament. In summary, biblical interpretation following the Reformation constituted a

---

10. Muller, *Post-Reformation Reformed Dogmatics*, 2:58.
11. Muller, *Post-Reformation Reformed Dogmatics*, 2:60.

significant break with medieval hermeneutics—but it was not a complete break.

Reformed Modifications to Biblical Interpretation

While the Reformation retained the Renaissance emphasis upon biblical exegesis in the original languages of Scripture, it also revived the medieval connection between exegesis and theology that Renaissance humanism had threatened to undermine. As Richard Muller noted, Reformed theologians attempted to maintain "the churchly tradition of theological exegesis as well as the critical labors of the textual scholar."[12] Even though the *quadriga* received varied attention in the medieval period, it had served as a vehicle for connecting the exposition of Scripture to the theology of the church. Doctrinal formulations are "a large step beyond exposition."[13] Reformed Protestants simultaneously inherited the concerns and questions that lay behind medieval theological formulation as well as the Renaissance emphasis on *ad fontes* (returning "to the sources"). In addition, while Reformed exposition of Scripture rested upon the literal sense of the text, exposition always aimed at the edification of the church.[14] This situation mandated a reformulation of proper biblical hermeneutics.

Reformed principles of biblical interpretation were both a correction and an expansion of earlier methods.

---

12. Muller, *Post-Reformation Reformed Dogmatics*, 2:61.

13. Muller, *Post-Reformation Reformed Dogmatics*, 2:442.

14. Muller, *Post-Reformation Reformed Dogmatics*, 2:443.

Typology was retained in Old Testament exposition based upon the example of Christ and His apostles, but careful rules were established in order to prevent abuses and outlandish allegorizing.[15] Scripture was compared with Scripture (*analogia scriptura*) in order to harmoniously understand the mind of the single divine Author of the Bible. Clearer passages were used in order to understand more obscure ones and passages that seemed, at first glance, to conflict with one another were woven together into theological formulation, often balancing two sides of the truth.[16] Allegory was largely rejected unless Scripture demanded it. With respect to the reference to Hagar and Sarah in Galatians 4, allegory was a necessary tool to connect the text to Christ. The same was true with respect to the Song of Solomon.[17] Even though there was one "literal" sense of the text of Scripture, doctrinal formulation

---

15. Muller, *Post-Reformation Reformed Dogmatics*, 2:453. See Knapp, "Understanding the Mind of God," 282–93. The regulation of typology continued to be a concern for Protestant theologians well after the period of Reformed orthodoxy had ended. For a very sober and useful example of this, see Fairbairn's *Typology of Scripture*.

16. These emphases are woven throughout the first chapter of the Westminster Confession of Faith, as is readily apparent even upon a cursory reading of the text.

17. An excellent example of the limited use of Reformed allegory and the principles upon which it was based is found in James Durham's exposition of the Song of Solomon, with an introduction by John Owen. Both Durham and Owen justify this method in their respective introductions. See James Durham, Clavis Cantici, *or, An Exposition of the Song of Solomon, with an Introduction by John Owen, D. D.* (London, 1668).

as well as application to the church demanded that various theological and practical conclusions could be legitimately drawn from that literal sense.[18] If the only thing a minister or commentator did was to give the people of God the proper literal and historical meaning of the Scriptures, then there would be no theology and no application in the sermon or commentary. In this sense, the *quadriga* did not entirely disappear in Reformed Protestantism. Instead it was "repositioned" within the literal sense and shifted into the realm of application.[19]

---

18. Muller, *Post-Reformation Reformed Dogmatics*, 2:473. In this connection Muller notes the importance of William Whitaker's *Disputations on Holy Scripture* for Protestant discussions of biblical interpretation in the seventeenth century. Trans. William Fitzgerald (1588; repr., Orlando, Fla.: Soli Deo Gloria, 2005), 482. Because this chapter is an introduction and summary only, I direct the reader to Muller for his wealth of primary-source evidence. Whitaker is cited elsewhere in this book.

19. Muller, *Post-Reformation Reformed Dogmatics*, 2:475, 479. Since the late eighteenth century, modern historical-critical exegesis has been concerned exclusively with the text itself and the meaning of the text in its historical setting. The result is that many modern commentaries are virtually devoid of theology and offer very little in the way of application to the church. Does this not tend to divorce the Bible from its divinely intended purpose to serve the church? In this connection, see David C. Steinmetz, "The Superiority of Precritical Exegesis," in *A Guide to Contemporary Hermeneutics: Major Trends in Biblical Interpretation*, ed. Donald K. McKim (Grand Rapids: Eerdmans, 1986), 65–77. While I do not agree with all of Steinmetz's conclusions concerning the *quadriga*, the primary value of his article lies in the observation that whereas critical exegesis is exclusively interested in the human author of Scripture and the historical context, pre-critical exegesis regarded God as the primary author of Scripture,

In addition, Reformed Protestants interpreted Scripture in terms of the analogy of faith (*analogia fidei*). The analogy of faith referred to the fact that the Bible must be interpreted in terms of an already-established body of doctrine. Initially this referred to the Apostles' Creed, the Lord's Prayer, and the Decalogue (as it had in the Middle Ages), but it eventually included the later catechisms and confessions of the church.[20] The analogy of faith was not regarded as a "creedal grid" received by tradition and to be imposed upon the text of Scripture, but it was viewed as an extended use of the analogy of Scripture.[21] In other words, one text of Scripture must not only harmonize with all other passages of Scripture, but its interpreters must also avoid reading a text in such a way that it contradicts the received body of doctrine that has been derived from Scripture.

In actuality, we use this practice often. For instance, if we believe on the basis of Romans 9 and Ephesians 1 that God sovereignly chooses some to everlasting life and passes by others, consigning them to eternal destruction, and that the elect only are the objects of God's saving love, we will not likely forget these established doctrines

---

finding significance in the text that transcends time. He concludes with the piercing observation that bare grammatical-historical exegesis will always be restricted to the academy, "where the question of truth can be endlessly deferred" (77). For the implications of this discussion with respect to preaching, see Ryan M. McGraw, "A Pastor's Analysis of Emphases in Preaching: Two False Dichotomies and Three Conclusions," *Puritan Reformed Journal* 2, no. 1 (January 2010): 266–76.

20. Muller, *Post-Reformation Reformed Dogmatics*, 2:493.

21. Muller, *Post-Reformation Reformed Dogmatics*, 2:494.

when we read in Ezekiel 18 that God has no pleasure in the death of the wicked. The idea is not to impose creedal formulations upon the text of Scripture, but rather to harmonize individual passages with the theology of the Bible as a whole, based on the assumption that those creedal formulations are proper expositions and summaries of Scripture. Exposition is the foundation of theology, but exposition is also helped and informed by theology. This does not place creedal documents above criticism, but it creates an interdependent hermeneutical spiral in which the exposition of Scripture is the foundation for theology and in which theology informs the exposition of Scripture.

This is where the question of good and necessary consequence becomes important. Reformed theologians, including the authors of the Westminster Confession, recognized that, unlike human authors, God is aware of all of the consequences of His words.[22] It is in light of this fact that good and necessary consequences ought to be deduced from the proper exposition of Scripture. Good and necessary consequence utilizes reason as properly applied to Scripture, but this does not mean that we are dealing with truth as derived from reason as opposed to truth as derived from Scripture. Instead, the principle allows the contemporary interpreter to apply an ancient text to a modern context.[23] When a necessary doctrine or application is legitimately drawn from the text of God's Word, then that

---

22. Muller, *Post-Reformation Reformed Dogmatics*, 2:498.

23. Muller, *Post-Reformation Reformed Dogmatics*, 2:499–500.

doctrine or application has the very power of the authority of God to enforce it. On the contrary, if good and necessary consequences are denied, then application is impossible. Moreover, Protestant interpreters recognized that doctrinal summaries drawn from Scripture—as well as contemporary application to the church—would become impossible without the principle of good and necessary consequence. As Muller observed, necessary consequence is one of the "final hermeneutical steps" used in order to formulate theology from Scripture.[24]

In summary, the principle of good and necessary consequence as set forth in the Westminster Confession of Faith represents the result of the Reformed Protestant quest to justify the task of theology and to apply the Scriptures in a contemporary context for the edification of the church. Reformed hermeneutics both built upon and amended medieval methods of biblical interpretation. The medieval *quadriga* was replaced by an emphasis upon the literal and historical sense of the text with doctrinal, practical, and christological applications drawn from that sense by good and necessary consequence. In large part, the entire Reformed tradition of doctrine and preaching hinges upon this point.

Historical Examples of the Principle
Even though the Westminster Assembly must be understood primarily as an English body, the divines held their

---

24. Muller, *Post-Reformation Reformed Dogmatics*, 2:501.

principles of biblical interpretation in common with the international Reformed tradition. For this reason, I will illustrate the principle both in its formulation and in its practice from two Scottish divines, George Gillespie and David Dickson.[25]

The Formulation of the Principle—George Gillespie

George Gillespie (1613–1648), a Scottish commissioner to the Westminster Assembly, provided one of the most thorough expositions and defenses of the principle of good and necessary consequence.[26] He observed in the first place that the Arminians demanded express proof texts alone to assert any doctrine or practice of Scripture. He responded by noting that without necessary consequences the Reformed church could not reject the errors of "Arians, Antitrinitarians, and Socinians."[27]

---

25. This material is illustrative only. Most of the relative primary sources for international Reformed theology on this point are buried in large Latin tomes. I have decided to omit references to these volumes here for the sake of simplicity and to ensure that this material remains accessible to a popular audience.

26. George Gillespie, *A Treatise of Miscellany Questions: Wherein Many Useful Questions and Cases of Conscience are Discussed and Resolved; for the Satisfaction of Those, Who Desire Nothing More, Than to Search for and Find out Precious Truths, in the Controversies of These Times* (University of Edinburgh, 1649), 238–45. Gillespie stated the doctrine in the following manner: "That necessary consequences from the written word of God, do sufficiently and strongly prove the consequent or conclusion, if theoretical, to be a certain divine truth which ought to be believed, and if practical, to be a necessary duty, which we are obliged unto, *jure Divino*."

27. Gillespie, *Miscellany Questions*, 238.

Good and necessary consequences drawn from Scripture do not make the truth rest upon reason. Reason is rather an instrument that is employed to draw legitimate conclusions from Scripture. A consequence of this kind "is not believed nor embraced by the strength of reason, but because it is the truth and will of God."[28] There is an important distinction, as well, between conclusions drawn from corrupted natural reason based upon mere human principles and the regenerate reason of Christians based upon scriptural and divine principles.[29]

Gillespie adds an important qualification at this stage of his treatment. There is a difference between legitimate consequences drawn from Scripture and necessary consequences drawn from Scripture.[30] This is a very important distinction. To illustrate Gillespie's point, the duty of

---

28. Gillespie, *Miscellany Questions*, 239.

29. For this reason, Thomas Aquinas was unwilling to refer to theology as a science in the same sense as other sciences: "It is seen that sacred doctrine is not a science. For every science proceeds from principles known from themselves [or, self-evident], but sacred doctrine proceeds from articles of faith, which are not known from themselves, nor are they submitted to by all, *for not all are of faith*, as is said in 2 Thess. 3. Therefore sacred doctrine is not a science." Thomas Aquinas, *Summa Theologica* (1274), q. 1, art. 2. Cited from http://www.corpusthomisticum.org/sth1001.html (translation mine). Reformed theologians such as Gillespie shared a common concern with some of the medieval doctors, such as Aquinas, to avert the charge that the use of reason in theology rooted theology in human reason rather than in the authority of Scripture.

30. Gillespie, *Miscellany Questions*, 240. Gillespie cites Aquinas to support this assertion.

personal daily Bible reading is a necessary consequence drawn from those statements in Scripture that describe the godly person as meditating upon the law of God day and night (Ps. 1:2), that commend the saints for searching the Scriptures daily (Acts 17:11), and that necessitate Bible reading for faith and godliness (2 Tim. 3:16). However, how much of the Bible Christians ought to read each day, the amount of time they spend upon it, and the hour(s) of the day that they use to read the Scriptures are legitimate applications (or consequences) that admit variable expressions. It is a necessary consequence that we must worship the God Triune on the Lord's Day, but the time of corporate worship is a legitimate consequence, or application. Such conclusions are "agreeable" to the principles of Scripture, but their precise form is not necessitated from Scripture.[31] If consequences drawn from Scripture are "necessary" as well as good, then they must carry the force of "Thus saith the Lord."

---

31. Gillespie, *Miscellany Questions*, 240. "Good and necessary consequence" is often confused in popular thought with what the Westminster Confession of Faith refers to as the "circumstances concerning the worship of God and government of the church" that may be ordered according to the "light of nature and Christian prudence," while still observing "the general rules of the word" (WCF 1.6). However, "necessary consequences" bear the full weight of divine authority, whereas "circumstances" are variable. In another place Gillespie asserted that "circumstances" must (1) be no substantial part of worship and bear no religious significance (e.g., when, where, how long, etc.); (2) cannot be determined by Scripture; and (3) must be necessary in order to carry out the commandments of God. Cited in Bannerman, *Church of Christ*, 1:349–60.

Gillespie provides biblical support for using good and necessary consequences, first by citing Christ's appropriation of the burning bush passage (see chapter 1), as well as by giving several more examples of the way in which the New Testament authors used the Old Testament.[32] Second, the law of God in the Old Testament was designed to be a summary of principles from which other applications should be derived by "good and necessary consequence."[33] Third, since the opinions of men are often refuted by showing them the consequences of their words, we must assume that the all-wise God is fully aware of the consequences of His words. To deny that the consequences of God's Word represent His will is "blasphemous," for, according to Gillespie, "This were to make the only wise God as foolish man, that cannot foresee all things which will follow from his words. Therefore we must needs hold, 'tis the mind of God which necessarily followeth from the words of God."[34] Fourth, if we deny the legitimacy of good and necessary consequence, then many absurdities will result, such as denying that women may come to the Lord's Supper.[35] Fifth, in reality, no one

---

32. Gillespie, *Miscellany Questions*, 240–41.

33. Gillespie, *Miscellany Questions*, 241–43. Gillespie uses the so-called laws of consanguinity (WCF 24.4) from Leviticus 18 as an example by illustrating that if sexual relationships are forbidden in one's direct lineage, then such relations are forbidden with great-grandchildren as well as with grandchildren, etc.

34. Gillespie, *Miscellany Questions*, 243.

35. Gillespie, *Miscellany Questions*, 244. He adds several similar examples.

is able to avoid using necessary consequences in theological discussions. All people must deduce conclusions from Scripture if they intend to make any assertions regarding what the Scriptures teach. Every controversy in the history of the church has been over "the sense of Scripture" rather than over its express statements.[36] Sixth, even civil magistrates deduce consequences from civil law in order to prove that a particular offense is in violation of the law, and "[we must not] deny to the Great God that which is a privilege of the little gods or magistrates."[37]

As Gillespie's treatment indicates, the principle of good and necessary consequence, whether expressed or implied in a confession of faith, is the vital foundation upon which such a confession rests. Letham wrote, "This is a profoundly important statement. It points to the need for continual thought in reading, preaching, and thinking about the Bible. It mandates theology. In order to begin to grasp the whole counsel of God, we need to be able to make legitimate deductions from the Bible.... In short, this chapter mandates systematic theology."[38] Whether

---

36. Gillespie, *Miscellany Questions*, 235. Even the Socinians, who denied good and necessary consequence in principle, were forced to use it in defense of their doctrines: "And generally it may be observed, that even they who most cry down consequences from Scripture, and call for express Scriptures, do notwithstanding, when themselves come to prove from Scripture their particular tenets, bring no other but consequential proofs. So far is wisdom justified, not only of her children, but even of her enemies."

37. Gillespie, *Miscellany Questions*, 245.

38. Letham, *Westminster Assembly*, 139. Later, Letham added that

Christians realize it or not, every time they cite a passage of Scripture in order to apply it to a particular doctrinal or practical matter, they are assuming that that text of Scripture necessarily implies the doctrine or practice in question. Westminster Confession 1.6 established the only solid ground upon which the Westminster Assembly could proceed with their work.

The Use of the Principle—David Dickson
David Dickson (1583–1662) was a Scottish minister who produced the first commentary on the Westminster Confession of Faith under the title *Truth's Victory over Error*.[39] Dickson's commentary on the Psalms provides many clear and concise examples of how the principle of good and necessary consequence was used to provide the seed thoughts of doctrine and application in seventeenth-century Reformed preaching. This work is not so much a commentary on the meaning of the text as it is a brief series of necessary consequences drawn from the proper exposition of the text,

---

exegesis and biblical theology alone are insufficient to define and to defend the Christian faith: "There is little doubt that biblical theology is a useful discipline, especially for the exegesis of passages in the Old Testament. However, by itself it is incapable of defending the church against heresy, since most heresies make use of biblical language and thus cannot be refuted by recourse to that alone" (245).

39. This work originated with Dickson's lectures at the University of Edinburgh in the 1650s. The circumstances surrounding its original publication are unclear and another author pirated it in the eighteenth century. It has been reprinted recently as David Dickson, *Truth's Victory over Error: An Exposition of the Westminster Confession of Faith* (Edinburgh: Banner of Truth, 2007).

which are largely assumed.[40] He drew a series of doctrinal and practical inferences from each verse of the text, followed by a citation of the portion of the text from which he drew each inference. This procedure is illustrated well by his observations on Psalm 2:7–8.[41]

At the time during which Dickson wrote his commentary, covenant theology was under significant development. In particular, the view of an eternal inter-trinitarian covenant of redemption between the Father and the Son was gaining wide acceptance. The concept of the covenant of redemption taught that, from eternity past, the Father made a covenant with the Son in which the Son agreed

---

40. Due to the nature of Dickson's commentary, the contrast that Knapp draws between Dickson and Owen is too strong. He argues that Dickson made the inferences drawn from Psalm 2 the primary meaning of the passage to the neglect of proper exegesis. Dickson's neglect of a full and explicit exegesis is better understood in light of the purpose of his commentary on the Psalms than it is in terms of an inconsistent application of Reformed exegetical rules. See Knapp, "Understanding the Mind of God," 223.

41. Examples of the use of good and necessary consequence in seventeenth-century theology are too numerous to list here. The eight principles of interpreting the Ten Commandments as set forth in Westminster Larger Catechism (WLC) Q. 99 provide one profound example. For the biblical foundations and application of these principles to the fourth commandment, see my *The Day of Worship: Reassessing the Christian Life in Light of the Sabbath* (Grand Rapids: Reformation Heritage Books, 2011), chap. 7. This chapter has been printed as a separate article, with some modifications, as "Principles of Sabbath Keeping: Jesus and Westminster," in *Puritan Reformed Journal* 3, no. 1 (January 2011): 316–27. Muller further explores the importance of good and necessary consequence in the covenant theology of the Westminster divines in Muller and Ward, *Scripture and Worship*, 59–82.

to become incarnate in order to purchase the redemption of the elect and to give to them the Holy Spirit.[42] This was an attempt to do justice to the implications of such texts as Titus 1:1–2, which describes the promise of eternal life occurring before time began. The covenant of redemption, which was eternal, served as the foundation to the covenant of grace, which was its historical outworking, including its application to believers. Although the covenant of redemption was not treated explicitly in the Westminster Confession or Catechisms, it was common for the Reformed orthodox of the seventeenth century to infer this teaching from texts such as Psalm 2:7–8.[43] This

---

42. For the development of covenant theology in the sixteenth and seventeenth centuries, see David A. Weir, *The Origins of Federal Theology in Sixteenth Century Reformation Thought* (Oxford: Clarendon Press, 1990); Lyle D. Bierma, "Law and Grace in Ursinus' Doctrine of the Natural Covenant," in *Protestant Scholasticism: Essays in Reassessment*, ed. Carl. R. Trueman and R. Scott Clark (Carlisle, UK: Paternoster Press, 2005), 96–110; Brian J. Lee, *Johannes Cocceius and the Exegetical Roots of Federal Theology* (Göttingen: Vandenhoeck and Ruprecht, 2009).

43. The "covenant of redemption" appears to be taught implicitly in Westminster Confession chap. 8, para. 1, which asserts, "It pleased God, in his eternal purpose, to choose and ordain the Lord Jesus, his only begotten Son, to be the Mediator between God and man." In this eternal purpose of God, the Son takes upon Himself the offices necessary to redeem His elect, and the Father promises to reward Him with a list of blessings in return. Significantly, the Savoy Declaration of Faith and Order adds "according to a covenant made between them both" immediately before "to be the Mediator" (Savoy Declaration, 8.1). For the development of the covenant of redemption in the seventeenth century, see Carl. R. Trueman, *John Owen: Reformed Catholic,*

is the necessary background for understanding Dickson's use of good and necessary consequence with reference to this psalm.

Dickson drew a series of eight inferences from these verses. First, based upon the words "I will declare the decree," the saints should take courage in times of persecution, since the stability of the church depends upon an eternal decree of God.[44] Second, because Christ is the eternal Word of the Father, He reveals "the secret counsel of the Trinity" ("I will declare the decree").[45] Third, Christ is a party of the eternal decree (covenant of redemption), and He receives the promises of the Father on behalf of the elect ("the LORD hath said unto me"). Fourth, the resurrection of Christ publicly proclaimed that he was the Son of God (Rom. 1:4) and that He fulfilled the office of Messiah particularly by His resurrection from the dead. At this stage, Dickson represents the Protestant concerns in biblical interpretation to do justice to the New Testament christological reading of the Old Testament. In the New Testament, the phrase "this day I have begotten thee" appears to refer to Christ's resurrection rather than to His eternal generation. Because the original context of the decree of God suggests an eternal transaction between

Renaissance Man (Burlington, Vt.: Ashgate, 2007), 82ff. Trueman brings out the peculiar importance of David Dickson in this development as well.

44. David Dickson, *A Commentary on the Psalms* (first published in three parts, 1653–1655; repr.; Edinburgh: Banner of Truth, 1959), 6–7.

45. Dickson, *Commentary on the Psalms*, 7.

the Father and the Son, Dickson asserts that the New Testament does not imply that Christ was begotten at the time of His resurrection, but rather that His resurrection was the ultimate declaration and completion of the eternal transaction between the Father and the Son.[46]

Fifth, the manifestation of the eternal plan of God through the finished work of Christ serves as a further ground of confidence for the church in spite of all opposition. This conclusion is derived from the fourth inference.[47] Sixth, following the declaration of the eternal purpose of God through His Son, the Son enlarges His kingdom through His work of intercession ("ask of me, and I will give thee the heathen" [Ps. 2:8]).[48] Seventh, the opposition of the nations will not be able to prevent the increasing expansion of Christ's kingdom, since the Father has promised that the nations will in fact be the heritage of His Son.[49] Lastly, if Christ is told to pray that the nations would be His inheritance, then, by inference, the church should also pray to this end in harmony with the Father and the Son.[50]

Not all examples of good and necessary consequence in Dickson's commentary are as complex as the one given

---

46. Dickson, *Commentary on the Psalms*, 7. For a similar but expanded treatment of this argument, see the Westminster divine Francis Cheynell (1608–1665), *The Divine Triunity of the Father, Son, and Holy Spirit* (London, 1650), 192–95.

47. Dickson, *Commentary on the Psalms*, 7–8.

48. Dickson, *Commentary on the Psalms*, 8.

49. Dickson, *Commentary on the Psalms*, 8.

50. Dickson, *Commentary on the Psalms*, 8.

here, but this instance illustrates well how the principle was put into practice and why it was so crucial. Do not all ministers struggle at some point with the question of how to preach Christ from the Old Testament? Do we not wrestle often with unraveling the manner in which Christ and His apostles interpreted the Old Testament? Do we not need to draw sermon applications directly from the text of Scripture in our preaching? Good and necessary consequence was the tool by which our forefathers in the Reformed faith accomplished these ends.

Conclusion

Good and necessary consequence is the foundation for understanding how the Westminster Assembly arrived at and constructed its theology. "The whole counsel of God" as it is revealed in Scripture cannot be discerned by a simplistic use of proof texts or by the bare exposition of Scripture. The fact that many Christians have objected to this principle of biblical interpretation explains why many readers on a popular level regard the proof texts of the Westminster Standards as an example of twisting Scripture to fit into a presupposed body of doctrine (like cramming a square peg into a round hole). However, when we approach the proof texts of these Standards, we ought to ask what implications the divines intended us to draw from the texts they have cited. Without good and necessary consequence, producing a confession of faith would have been an impossible task. By means of this principle, the Westminster divines sought to sit at the feet of Jesus Christ and learn from His own use of Scripture. The Westminster Confession of Faith and the Larger and Shorter Catechisms are evidence that they learned from their Master well.

3

Its Importance

Not only do the Scriptures require the principle of good and necessary consequence, but its great importance has also been reflected in the theology and practice of the church throughout the centuries. The previous chapter's historical section has demonstrated this fact to some degree, but it is particularly true with respect to the christological and trinitarian formulations produced in the first five centuries of the church. In addition, this principle holds important implications for corporate worship and the sacraments. These instances will demonstrate the vital necessity of good and necessary consequence for the well-being of the church and, at points, even its existence.

The Doctrine of the Person of Christ

Orthodox Protestant denominations today assume the validity of the principle of good and necessary consequence with respect to the doctrine of the person of the Lord Jesus Christ. Near the end of the fourth century and the beginning of the fifth, the church affirmed through her creeds that the Lord Jesus Christ is both truly God and truly man, and that these two natures are not mixed or confused, but that each nature retains the properties belonging to it. Although the Lord Jesus is fully God and fully man, these two distinct natures are found in one personality only, so that the Lord may truly be said to be the God-man. These conclusions arose in the midst of controversy and were posed in response to the doctrines of Arianism. Arius and his followers asserted that the Lord Jesus was not of the *same* substance with the Father (*homoousios*), but was only *like* the Father (*homoiousios*).[1] His position rested upon the fact that the Scriptures did not *explicitly* state that Jesus and the Father were of the same substance. On the other hand, the Scriptures clearly taught that the Lord Jesus Christ was a true human being.[2]

---

1. For the historical development and biblical foundations of the doctrine of Christ's person, see Herman Bavinck, *Reformed Dogmatics*, ed. John Bolt, trans. John Vriend (Grand Rapids: Baker, 2004), 223–322 and Donald MacLeod, *The Person of Christ* (Westmont, Ill.: InterVarsity, 1998).

2. Bannerman, *Church of Christ*, 2:409. I do not mean to suggest that the christological controversies ought to be thought of simplistically in terms of the Arian controversy alone. The teachings of Eutyches, Nestorius, and Appolonarius, as well as the rulings of several subsequent church councils, all have bearing on the final shape in which the church formulated the doctrine of the person of Christ. I have cut out most of the material for the sake of simplicity in order to illustrate the point at hand. For more information see J. N. D. Kelly, *Early Christian Doctrines* (New York: HarperCollins, 1960). For a sketch of the complex history of further developments in Christology, see Robert Letham, *Union with Christ: In Scripture, History, and Theology* (Phillipsburg, N.J.: P&R, 2011), 23–35.

The creedal responses of the church did not result from citing mere proof texts. In addition to express statements affirming Christ's deity, such as Romans 9:5 and 1 John 5:20, the church used a series of inferences to demonstrate that He was divine. They used passages that showed Jesus accepting worship and others that ascribed divine attributes and knowledge to Him.[3] However, they maintained with equal vigor the statements in Scripture asserting the humanity of Jesus: He grew weary and had to sleep, eat, and drink. Even though, as God, He knows all things, Jesus referred to some things that were beyond his knowledge (e.g., Mark 13:32). These two facts cannot coexist without asserting full deity and full humanity in the same person. On the one hand, the Scriptures assert that the Lord Jesus Christ is the Lord of heaven and earth and the One through whom and for whom all things were made (Col. 1:16) and who upholds all things by the word of his power (Heb. 1:3). On the other hand, He was a helpless infant who was carried in the womb of the Virgin Mary. He was made like man in all ways, sin only excepted (Heb. 4:15; Rom. 8:3). The church correctly concluded that if Jesus lacked or lost any aspect of deity, then, by definition, He was not divine. However, if His humanity

---

3. The Westminster Larger Catechism would later provide a useful summary of these criteria: "Q. 11. How doth it appear that the Son and the Holy Ghost are God equal with the Father? A. The Scriptures manifest that the Son and the Holy Ghost are God equal with the Father, ascribing unto them such names, attributes, works, and worship, as are proper to God only."

possessed divine attributes, then He would not be truly human. For these reasons, the Nicene Creed, the Athanasian Creed, and particularly the Definition of Chalcedon have consistently asserted the sentiments expressed well by the Westminster Shorter Catechism (WSC): "The only Redeemer of God's elect is the Lord Jesus Christ, who, being the eternal Son of God, became man, and so was, and continueth to be, God and man, in two distinct natures, and one person forever" (Q. 21).

The doctrine of the two natures of Christ requires a broad knowledge of Scripture and a capable application of its principles. What is more necessary for God's glory and man's salvation than to understand correctly the person and work of the Savior? This is not the paltry quibbling of theologians detached from the realities of the lives and needs of the people. Jesus Christ asserted that if men did not identify Him with Jehovah, they would die in their sins (John 8:21, cf. vv. 58–59). The author of Hebrews insisted that in order to satisfy the wrath of God on behalf of His people, our great High Priest had to be a partaker "of flesh and blood" and be made like us in every way, "yet without sin" (Heb. 2:14, 17; 4:15). The Christ needed to be God, since only the sacrifice of His infinitely righteous person could sufficiently pay the debt of man's sin and bear the infinite weight of the wrath of God on the cross. Yet without true humanity, He could not stand in the place of His people as the second Adam (Rom. 5:13–18; 1 Cor. 15:22) and bring them righteousness and life in place of the sin and death brought by the first Adam.[4] If Jesus' humanity were more than human, and if His deity were less than divine, then not a single soul could be redeemed. This conclusion is neither esoteric nor allegorical, but inescapable and vital. Yet the biblical data concerning the person of the Lord Jesus Christ can be harmonized only through a careful use of good and necessary consequence.

The Doctrine of the Triune Nature of God

Perhaps the most fundamental and commonly accepted doctrine among various Christian denominations is that of the triune nature of God.[5] The doctrine of the Trinity

---

4. Westminster Larger Catechism questions 38–40 contain a peerless statement as to why our Mediator had to be God, man, and both together in one person. See the Scriptures cited therein for more detail.

5. I present simply the briefest sketch of the biblical data relevant to the Trinity here. For two useful contemporary defenses of the doctrine of the Trinity, see Robert Letham, *The Holy Trinity: In Scripture, History, Theology, and Worship* (Phillipsburg, N.J.: P&R, 2004) and Peter Toon, *Our Triune God: A Biblical Portrayal of the Trinity* (Vancouver: Regent College Publishing, 1996). Since much of the evidence for the doctrine of the Trinity comes from the gospel of John, see also Andreas J. Kostenberger and Scott R. Swain, *Father, Son, and Spirit: The Trinity and John's Gospel* (Westmont, Ill.: InterVarsity, 2008). However, because Kostenberger and Swain are primarily concerned with biblical theology rather than systematic and historical theology, their treatment suffers from limitations in the areas of systematic and historical theology. For a treatment of the centrality of the Trinity in systematic theology, see Douglas F. Kelly, *Systematic Theology*, vol. 1, *Grounded in Holy Scripture and Understood in Light of the Church: The God Who Is; The Holy Trinity* (Ross-shire, UK: Christian Focus, 2008). On the flaws in this work, see my review in *Westminster Theological Journal* 72, no. 1 (Spring 2010): 193–97.

is the cardinal example of the vital importance of properly applying the principle of good and necessary consequence. The doctrine of the Trinity is defined concisely in Shorter Catechism Q. 6: "There are three persons in the Godhead; the Father, and the Son, and the Holy Ghost; and these three are one God, the same in substance, equal in power and glory." It is a fundamental assumption in the Bible is that there is one true God (Deut. 6:4; 1 Cor. 8:4; WSC Q. 5). Yet the Scriptures clearly assert that the Father, Son, and Holy Spirit each are God. These three divine persons are distinct from one another. The simultaneous appearance of all three persons at the baptism of Jesus, for instance, demonstrates this (Matt. 3:16–17). Jesus prayed to the Father in John 17, and the sending of the Holy Spirit is ascribed to both the Father and the Son (John 14:16; 15:26). Each of the three persons is God, yet there is only one God. Each of the three persons has a distinct personality and fulfills a distinct purpose in the accomplishment and application of the redemption. How can we harmonize the teaching of passages such as these?

Although man is infinitely beneath his Creator and cannot comprehend the triune nature of God, the historic doctrine of the Trinity alone does justice to all of the biblical evidence. The Scriptures cannot teach that there is one God and three Gods any more than it can teach that God is one person and three persons. The necessary consequence accepted by nearly all Christian churches throughout the centuries has been that God is one in essence and three in persons, who are neither three separate beings nor one being manifesting Himself in three different roles. This doctrine has always separated true branches of the church from those that have apostatized from the faith that was once for all delivered to the saints (Jude 3). All who assert the triune nature of God assume the indispensable necessity of good and necessary consequence. The very being of the church depends upon it.

The doctrine of the Trinity is perhaps the most complex example of the principle of good and necessary consequence. However, as W. G. T. Shedd wrote, "Those churches which have followed Scripture most implicitly, and have most feared human speculation, are the very churches which have inserted into their creeds the most highly analytic statement that has yet been made of the doctrine of the Trinity."[6]

Worship

The doctrines of the two natures of Christ and the trinity of God demonstrate that the church has depended upon the principle of good and necessary consequence in its most fundamental theological formulations. However, this principle is vital in many other areas of theology and practice. Good and necessary consequence is especially important in determining which worship practices are demanded in Scripture. When the church either neglects or denies good and necessary consequence, she runs the

---

6. W. G. T. Shedd, introduction to *Augustine on the Trinity*, in *Nicene and Post-Nicene Fathers*, ed. Philip Schaff, 1st series (1887; repr., Peabody, Mass: Hendrickson, 2004), 3:3.

risk of violating the sanctity of corporate worship by taking away from God's commandments (Deut. 12:32).

This is evident in the account of the death of Nadab and Abihu, the two sons of Aaron, in Leviticus 10:1–3. After having already enjoyed great privileges and blessings among God's people, Nadab and Abihu received the honor of being consecrated as priests. At the end of chapter 9, fire came down from heaven and consumed the sacrifices of the altar. Chapter 10 begins with Nadab and Abihu approaching God in their first act of priestly service. This was simultaneously their first and their last act in the priesthood. As they brought their censers filled with fire to worship the Lord, the same fire from heaven that had previously consumed the sacrifices burst forth from the altar and consumed the priests. The nature of their sin was stated plainly: they offered "strange [or profane] fire" before the Lord, and they offered that "which he commanded them not" (v. 1). Whatever else was true about this "strange fire," the only fault emphasized in the text was that it was not accepted because God had not commanded it.

This example is significant because there is no place in the law prior to this point in which the priests were given an explicit command that they should offer one kind of fire only. God had never directly *forbidden* the priests from offering more than one kind of fire. At that time, He had not even expressly *commanded* what kind of fire was acceptable in his sight. Yet the charge that they offered fire "which he commanded them not" justified the death penalty. When readers ignore the chapter divisions, the text gives the impression that Nadab and Abihu were to infer the will of God from His immediately preceding actions. The Lord testified His good pleasure toward the consecration of the priesthood and of the altar, which had been done according to His commandments, by sending supernatural fire out of heaven to consume the sacrifices (Lev. 9:24). This fire was to be kept perpetually burning thereafter. Jeremiah Burroughs (1600–1646), who was a member of the Westminster Assembly, observed, "They should have reasoned thus with themselves: 'Has God let fire come down from heaven upon the altar, and has he commanded that it should be preserved on the altar for his service? Surely this must be God's mind, then, that we should make use of this fire than any other fire.'"[7] The failure to draw a good and necessary consequence from God's action proved fatal in this case.

God treated Nadab and Abihu as though the necessary consequences of His words and actions were as binding on the worship practices of His people as His explicit commands. As Burroughs reminded his readers:

> I have told you before that in matters of worship we must have warrant from the Word, but it does not follow that we must have a direct, express warrant in everything. As it is many times in some kind of picture, the great art is in the cast of the looks. You cannot say it's in the drawing of this line or the other

---

7. Jeremiah Burroughs, *Gospel Worship*, ed. Don Kistler (1648; repr., Morgan, Pa.: Soli Deo Gloria, 1990), 18.

line, but altogether. It is in the cast of the looks that causes the beauty of the picture. So in the Scripture you cannot say that this one line or another proves it, but let them all be laid together and there will be a kind of aspect of God's mind. We may see that this is the mind of God rather than the other, and we are bound to go that way.[8]

If this principle is excluded, many commonly accepted elements of worship would be excluded with it. There would be no warrant for practices such as the call to worship, the use of baptism in worship, the offering, and the benediction without the use of good and necessary consequence.[9] Denying necessary consequences would even exclude women from partaking of the Lord's Supper, since there is no express command or example indicating that they should do so! If the only ground for excluding certain practices of worship is that there is no *express* command in Scripture for them, then the church will inevitably offend her Lord by omitting parts of His revealed will, as did Nadab and Abihu. However, if the church continues to include them in spite of having any Scriptural grounds for them, then she will still be guilty of the sin of Nadab and Abihu as well, by knowingly offering what God has not commanded.

If we object that this was an Old Testament principle of interpretation no longer applicable to the church today,

---

8. Burroughs, *Gospel Worship*, 19.

9. For the Scriptural warrant for each of these elements in corporate worship, see McGraw, "Consequences of Reformed Worship."

then we must ask whether or not this principle is similar to the procedure that Jesus used to confute the Sadducees. The church has continued to use some of her elements of worship merely out of custom for far too long, thus doing the right things for the wrong reasons. The church cannot afford to be without biblical warrant for any of the elements of worship. It does little good to have biblical elements of worship if the church does not include them on the grounds that they are biblical. While God does not execute the death penalty upon His people every time they fail to worship him perfectly, it is to the church's detriment—and, at times, to her peril—if she does not pursue the logical consequences of the will of God as it is revealed in Scripture. The weight of this responsibility falls most heavily upon those who have been charged with the ministry of God's Word and with leading the public worship of God. Good and necessary consequences are indispensable for the practice of biblical worship.

Sacraments

There is one other illustration that is worth mentioning. At least tacitly (that is, with regard to the Trinity and the two natures of Christ), most Reformed Baptists admit that some things necessary to faith and practice are not only expressly set down in Scripture, but are rather deduced from it by good and necessary consequence.[10]

---

10. For example, the London Baptist Confession of Faith of 1689, which was intentionally modeled after the Westminster Confession, asserts that all things necessary to God's glory, salvation,

However, although Baptists admit inferences and deductions with regard to the Trinity, they often rule them out as a matter of course with regard to the question of paedobaptism. Baptists often demand either one definite example of infant baptism in the New Testament or an express command to baptize children. This places

---

faith, and life are either "expressly set down or necessarily contained in Holy Scripture" (1.6). The phrase "necessarily contained" appears to be synonymous with "good and necessary consequence," since both terms are contrasted with the "express" statements of Scripture. Rowland Ward points out that since the London Confession was in other respects modeled after the Westminster Confession and altered its language only when it provoked disagreement, its authors must have intended to reject "good and necessary consequence." See Muller and Ward, *Scripture and Worship*, 97. So with J. V. Fesko, *Word, Water, and Spirit: A Reformed Perspective on Baptism* (Grand Rapids: Reformation Heritage Books, 2010), 148, n. 61. This observation should be duly weighed. However, the statement may not necessarily be corrective. It may have been changed to strengthen the assertion that doctrines and practices that are deduced properly from Scripture possess full divine authority because they are "necessarily contained" in Scripture. This is at least how Baptist theologian Samuel Waldron has understood this change: "The phrase, 'or necessarily contained in the Holy Scripture' is equivalent to the phrase in the Westminster Confession it is intended to clarify: 'or by good and necessary consequence may be deduced from Scripture.' What may be by sound logic deduced from Scripture, that is to say, what is necessarily contained in it, has the authority of Scripture itself." Samuel E. Waldron, *A Modern Exposition of the 1689 Baptist Confession of Faith* (Webster, N.Y.: Evangelical Press, 2005), 42–43. This matter deserves more research in the primary sources, but in light of the fact that rejecting necessary consequence in the seventeenth century was ordinarily associated with heresy, it seems unlikely that the Baptists would have desired to risk such an association. For more on this point, see chapter 4.

an unbiblical limitation upon the discussion. Have not Socinians and other Unitarians consistently rejected the doctrine of the Trinity on these same grounds? It would be more proper to say that if the doctrine of infant baptism were required from Scripture by good and necessary consequence, then it ought to be believed and practiced just as much as if it has been revealed by express command or approved example.

This is not the place for a biblical defense of infant baptism, but a brief summary of the argument in its favor illustrates the point at hand.[11] The case for baptizing the children of believers rests primarily upon the essential unity of the covenant of grace in the Old and New Testaments, as well as the fact that baptism has replaced circumcision as the sign of that same covenant (Col. 2:11–12). God commanded that the infants of believers should receive the sign of the covenant, and He has never revoked this command, even though the sign has been changed from circumcision to baptism. Peter's appeal in Acts 2:38–39 ("Repent, and be baptized every one of you in the name of Jesus Christ for the remission of sins.... For the promise is unto you, and

---

11. In my opinion, the three best treatments of paedobaptism are Pierre Marcel, *The Biblical Doctrine of Infant Baptism: Sacrament of the Covenant of Grace*, trans. Philip Edgcumbe Hughes (1951; New York: Westminster Publishing House, 2000); Bannerman, *Church of Christ*; and John Calvin, *Institutes of the Christian Religion*, ed. John T. McNeill, trans. Ford Lewis Battles (Philadelphia: Westminster Press, 1960), 4.8.16. Out of the flood of literature on the sacrament of baptism, one of the most thorough and helpful treatments from a Reformed perspective is Fesko's, *Word, Water, and Spirit*.

to your children, and to all that are afar off, even as many as the LORD our God shall call") is almost an exact parallel with the covenant of circumcision given to Abraham in Genesis 17:4, 7: "My covenant is with thee, and thou shalt be a father of many nations…. And I will establish my covenant between me and thee and thy seed after thee in their generations for an everlasting covenant, to be a God unto thee, and to thy seed after thee." The inference from all of this is that, just as infants received circumcision, which was the seal of the righteousness that comes by faith and of the circumcision of the heart (Rom. 2:28–29, 4:11; Deut. 10:16; Jer. 4:4), so the infants of believers should continue to be counted as heirs of the promises under the new covenant sign of baptism. Both circumcision and baptism are spiritual signs and seals of faith, given to a spiritual people, in the context of the spiritual covenant of grace.

It is one matter if a Baptist denies that paedobaptism is a necessary consequence of the teaching of Scripture, but to deny the validity of paedobaptism solely on the grounds that there are no explicit examples of it in the New Testament is, in principle, the same thing as denying the Trinity on the grounds that there are no explicit passages in which it is set forth. If our Baptist brethren reject good and necessary consequence as a category for argumentation in this one case, then, in order to be consistent, they must deny it in every other case as well.[12]

---

12. My point in this section is to address principles rather than doctrine. However, the assertion that the only New Testament examples of baptism involve adults who have made professions of faith is not

In his defense of the practice of infant baptism, Pierre Marcel pointedly remarked, "In theology, that which follows by legitimate deductions from Scriptural norms is as exact as that which is explicitly stated.... Were it not so, the exercise of the pastoral ministry, the cure of souls, preaching, discipline, and so on would be absolutely impossible!"[13] This statement serves as a general conclusion to all that has been said in this chapter. Good and necessary consequence is important not only with regard to doctrines over which godly Christians may disagree (such as the question of who ought to be baptized), but it is also foundational to some of the fundamental tenets of the Christian faith, as well as to the practices of worship. As Bannerman summarized:

> It is evidently both unwarrantable and perilous to lay down as a canon of Scripture interpretation, that whenever there is no express and explicit injunction, in so many words, requiring a duty to be performed, there the deed is unlawful, or at least not commanded. It is unwarrantable; because we have no right to limit God as to the forms in which he may be pleased to make known to us his will, if, in one form or another, it is made known. It is perilous as regards

---

entirely accurate. The household baptisms of Acts 16 and 1 Corinthians 1 fit the Old Testament practice of household circumcision, which explicitly included infants, better than the Baptist explanation. Was it possible for a first-century Jewish Christian to understand these things in any other way than as a continuation of the manner in which God had already dealt with His people for thousands of years?

13. Marcel, *Biblical Doctrine of Infant Baptism*, 189–90.

ourselves; because there can be no more dangerous position than to assume the attitude of refusing to regard the will of God intimated to us, because it is not intimated in a manner which we may consider to be the plainest at best.[14]

---

14. Bannerman, *Church of Christ*, 2:101. Incidentally, the legitimacy of systematic theology as a discipline stands or falls upon the principle of good and necessary consequences. See Richard B. Gaffin, "The Vitality of Reformed Systematic Theology," in *The Faith Once Delivered: Essays in Honor of Wayne R. Spear*, ed. Anthony T. Selvaggio (Phillipsburg, N.J.: P&R, 2007), 29.

4

Objections

The idea of good and necessary consequence has been attacked since the earliest centuries of the Christian church. The three primary objections to this principle are that (1) doctrines derived from it cannot be binding upon the consciences of believers, (2) it makes the faith and practice of believers dependent upon the rationalizations of men rather than upon the Word of God, and (3) it takes the Bible out of the hands of the people and places it into the hands of experts who act as a priesthood between the believer and the Scriptures.[1]

---

1. Objections to the principle also result from many modern students of the Bible assuming principles of exegesis that are based upon modern standards of scholarship rather than upon the examples found in Scripture. Early Reformed theologians attempted to apply the sufficiency of Scripture to all areas of theological study, including hermeneutics. While modern exegesis focuses almost *exclusively* on the historical meaning of Scripture, early Reformed writers, including the Westminster divines, though placing heavy emphasis upon the historical meaning of Scripture, focused on the theological interpretation of Scripture as well. See chapter 2 for more detail.

Necessary Consequences Cannot Be Binding

Walter Kaiser represents the first two of these objections well:

> To bind the consciences of believers to that which is not *directly* taught in Scripture is perilously close to raising up a new form of tradition that vies for equal recognition with Scripture itself. We rightly object when cults and sects add to the Scriptures merely human ideas. We should likewise protest when the human interpretations of the Bible are raised to the level of Scripture. Moreover, such inference is an infringement on our liberty in Christ.[2]

Kaiser here refers to any doctrine or command that is not derived from explicit statements of Scripture. He implies that to formulate doctrines or practices by deductions or inferences in any case is to set aside the commandments of God, teaching as doctrines the commandments of men (Matt. 15:9). In Kaiser's view, inferences are not good or necessary consequences, but "merely human ideas." His concerns are partially valid. God alone is the Lord of the conscience, and He has left it free from the doctrines and commandments of men.[3]

---

2. Walter Kaiser and Moises Silva, *An Introduction to Biblical Hermeneutics* (Grand Rapids: Zondervan, 1994), 204, emphasis mine.

3. Cf. Westminster Confession 20.2. For a useful exposition of Christian liberty in relation to the Law of God, see Samuel Bolton (1606–1654), *The True Bounds of Christian Freedom, or a Treatise wherein the Rights of the Law Are Vindicated, the Liberties of Grace Maintained, and the Several Late Opinions against the Law Are Examined and Confuted* (London, 1656).

Each man shall stand or fall before his own master (Rom. 14:4). Jesus Himself pronounced His strongest indictments against those who elevated the traditions of men to the level of the Word of God, and Christians must be zealous against such dangerous errors. They must always plead with God to deliver them from falling into such deceptions. However, it is easy to gather from what has already been said that Kaiser's assertion is not only contrary to the example set by Jesus and His apostles, but that it would rule out the fundamental doctrines of the incarnation of Christ and the Holy Trinity. It is strange that Kaiser should make such strong assertions, since he is an orthodox Protestant who holds these doctrines as dear to his heart and as fundamental to the faith. If Kaiser were to be consistent, then he would be forced to agree that the doctrine of the Trinity could not be binding upon anyone. It is "not directly taught in Scripture" and would therefore be, in his words, "perilously close to raising up a new tradition that vies for equal recognition with Scripture itself."

Kaiser's reference to "cults and sects" as guilty of adding to the Scriptures is somewhat ironic. He has in view groups such as the Mormons, who have added their own books and teachings to the books of the Bible. Yet, as Bannerman noted, "The challenge has been thrown down again and again by *heretics* in all ages: 'Give us an express text of Scripture contradicting our views and asserting yours. We refuse to submit to mere human inferences in place of Scripture statement.'"[4] Such heresies included Arianism and its derivatives, as well as Socinianism and other forms of antitrinitarianism.[5] Many sects have in fact been guilty of adding "merely human ideas" to the teaching of Scripture. Historically, however, the rejection of good and necessary consequence has not been a hallmark of orthodoxy, but rather a hallmark of heresy. Furthermore, it is questionable whether Kaiser's comparison to the practices of cults and sects is proper in any respect. These cults and sects frequently fail (or do not even attempt) to deduce their own doctrines exclusively from the Scriptures. They often claim an infallible interpretation of Scripture that cannot be reproduced by those who are not initiated into their groups. More commonly, they claim a supplemental form of revelation that is viewed as superior to the Bible and upon which they rest the bulk of their claims. Some cults, such as the Mormons, refuse to admit Scripture consequences to the point of denying the simple deduction that since

---

4. Bannerman, *Church of Christ*, 2:409, emphasis mine. It is interesting to read Turretin at this point, since he argues that Scripture consequences are primarily to be used in formulating theology through the negative task of refuting error. This principle, in a sense, is the foundation of his entire work, which is designed to be an "elenctic" theology, or a theology that attempts to teach truth by refuting erroneous positions.

5. For more on Socinianism, see Joel L. Heflin, "Omnipotent Sweetness? Puritanism Versus Socinianism," *Puritan Reformed Journal* 1, no. 2 (July 2009): 64–95, and especially Philip Dixon, *Nice and Hot Disputes: The Doctrine of the Trinity in the Seventeenth Century* (London: T&T Clark, 2003).

Jesus accepted divine worship, He was God equal with the Father.

Moreover, since Jesus Himself both used and required the principle of good and necessary consequence, it cannot be "an infringement on our liberty in Christ," as Kaiser has asserted. If *illegitimate* inferences are drawn from Scripture and are made binding upon the consciences of men, then it is an infringement upon their liberty of conscience. However, this is not the same as saying that inferences inherently violate the liberty of Christ's people. What kind of "liberty" does Kaiser intend to preserve? Apparently, it is liberty to believe and obey only what is directly stated in Scripture and to reject freely the deductions and inferences necessitated by the text. Yet does the Christian then have the liberty to ignore the example of Christ and His apostles in their use of Scripture? If Christ and His apostles cannot serve as a model for biblical interpretation, then does *this* not place us at the mercy of a model that is derived from mere human invention? Does this not also deny the assumption made by the New Testament that apostolic exegesis was meant to be convincing to an unbelieving audience? Does the Christian have the liberty to reject Jesus' careful selection of the burning bush passage to prove the doctrine of the resurrection? Does the Christian have the liberty to reject the doctrines of the incarnation and the Trinity? True Christian liberty is a freedom from the condemning power of the law and from the eternal death resulting from it. The Christian's liberty is a liberty to obey God freely and in voluntary service, joyfully submitting to His will in gratitude for the grace of the gospel. The liberty of the Christian is *not* a liberty to reject the will of God as it is revealed in Scripture, regardless of the form in which that will is revealed.

Necessary Consequences Found Faith upon Reason Instead of Scripture

Another objection is that the principle of good and necessary consequence makes the faith of believers dependent upon the rationalizations of men rather than upon the Word of God. This objection has been raised for centuries. Many argue that if doctrines are derived from the Bible through the use of reason, then they rest upon human authority rather than upon the authority of the Word of God. This objection is ordinarily the foundation of the objection that inferences from Scripture cannot be binding upon the consciences of men. The most obvious flaw with this objection is that every formulation of doctrine is obtained through a process of reason and deduction, whether from express statements of Scripture or otherwise. Forming theological conclusions does not make reason the foundation of faith and theology any more than observing and describing the natural world makes man the creator of the world. In fact, the words of Scripture have no meaning unless men draw conclusions from them. As William Whitaker (1548–1595) wrote, "The Scripture consists not in the bare words, but in the sense, interpretation, and meaning of the words."[6] The role of reason is not to *create* theology from reading Scripture. Reason is a necessary tool that is used to *receive* the doctrines already stated and implied in the Holy Word of God. Warfield aptly noted that "if [this] plea is valid at all, it destroys at once our confidence in all doctrines, no one of which is ascertained without the aid of human logic."[7] In a sense, the defense of the principle of good and necessary consequence is identical with the defense of the study of systematic theology, which is rejected by many on these same grounds.[8]

Necessary Consequences Take the Bible Away from the People

The third objection against the principle of good and necessary consequence is that it takes the Bible out of the hands of the average person in the church and places it in the hands of experts. This is a serious charge, since Scripture declares itself to be both necessary and sufficient

6. William Whitaker, *Disputations on Holy Scripture*, trans. William Fitzgerald (1588; repr., Orlando, Fla.: Soli Deo Gloria Publications, 2005), 402.

7. Warfield, "Westminster Doctrine," 227. The last several pages of this section of Warfield's helpful article are composed of several useful block quotations regarding this principle, beginning with Aquinas but especially extracted from the writings of the Westminster divines.

8. For a useful defense of systematic theology as a discipline, see B. B. Warfield, "The Right of Systematic Theology," in *Selected Shorter Writings of Benjamin B. Warfield*, ed. John E. Meeter (Phillipsburg, N.J.: P&R Publications, 1970), 219–79.

for salvation through faith in Jesus Christ as well as to make the man of God complete and thoroughly equipped for every good work (2 Tim. 3:16–17). However, even though all believers may understand the Scriptures sufficiently for salvation as the Spirit of God applies the Word to their hearts, not all believers will understand all things in the Bible equally.[9] With regard to gifts, all men are not created equal. Each redeemed person has different abilities by nature as well as different gifts by grace. This diversity is not a result of defects in individual believers but is a part of the wise plan of God for His people. Among the gifts Christ gave for the well-being of His people after He ascended into heaven were those suited to making men "pastors and teachers" (Eph. 4:11). Through gifting certain men to teach, God's purpose is that they should prevent His people from being "children…tossed to and fro, and carried about with every wind of doctrine" (v. 14). This affirms that unless Christ had gifted some men to labor in the Word and doctrine in order to understand and teach the Scriptures to His people, then they would be subject to every sort of error, as unstable as a tumultuous sea blasted by powerful winds.

---

9. See Westminster Confession 1.7: "All things in Scripture are not alike plain in themselves, nor alike clear unto all, yet those things which are necessary to be known, believed, and observed for salvation are so clearly propounded, and opened in some place of Scripture or other, that not only the learned, but the unlearned, in a due use of the ordinary means, may attain unto a sufficient understanding of them."

Does this mean, however, that the faith of believers depends upon fallible human instruments and that men are lords over others' consciences? Certainly it does not. Paul commended the Berean Christians because they "searched the Scriptures" (Acts 17:11). Yet what is often overlooked is that they searched the Scriptures in response to the preaching of Paul and Silas in the synagogue (v. 10). The Berean model teaches us to test what we hear from those who have been gifted to understand and to preach the Scriptures. An individual's reading of the Bible must not be detached from the teaching and preaching of the Bible. That believers need teachers to help them better understand the full meaning of Scripture does not mean that they are deficient in faith or intellectually impoverished; rather, Christ gave pastors and teachers to His church for their well-being. Christians are designed by the Holy Spirit to possess some gifts and abilities and to lack others so that they might thrive together as an interdependent body. Whitaker gave the following counsel on the use of gifted Christian teachers: "We may use their labors, advice, prudence, and knowledge; but we should use them always cautiously, modestly, and discreetly, and so as still to retain our own liberty."[10]

By nature and by grace, God has designed His people to be dependent upon one another. This includes those who teach as much as those who are taught. Pierre Marcel asserted correctly "that every believer, whoever he may

---

10. Whitaker, *Disputations on Holy Scripture*, 473.

be, cannot live alone the life of faith by remaining within the narrow framework of his own subjectivity and that he must actively take part in the Church, a divine institution, is a decree which depends upon the nature of the gospel and the work of Christ as much as on the nature of man."[11] When a man or woman is converted and joins the church, it is not likely that he or she will immediately understand doctrines such as the two natures of Christ or the Trinity very well. He or she may have great confusion as to how to piece together what the Scriptures reveal concerning these doctrines. After all, it took the church several centuries in the face of much false teaching to define these doctrines precisely. Good teachers will teach people these doctrines and direct them to the Scriptures in which they must be found. Learning the doctrines of Scripture is like learning a new language. Through a gradual process, what was once foreign or obscure gradually becomes clear and easy though use.[12] Teachers in the church will not be correct at every point. However, according to God's Word, it is possible to need teachers to instruct us in obscure matters without making our faith dependent upon them.[13] By

---

11. Pierre Marcel, *The Relevance of Preaching*, ed. William Childs Robinson, trans. Rob Roy McGregor (Grand Rapids: Baker, 1963), 21.

12. See my article, "Retaining Scripture in Our Minds and in Our Hearts," where I expand the manner in which we ought to grow in our knowledge and understanding of the Scriptures. *Katechomen: The Online Journal of Greenville Presbyterian Theological Seminary*, April 1, 2010: http://katekomen.gpts.edu/2010/04/retaining-scripture-in-our-minds-and-in.html.

13. Several passages of Scripture are relevant to this discussion.

God's wisdom, the Scriptures are both obscure enough to require explanation and clear enough to be understood through proper instruction. Let us pray through our studies of Scripture, and let us use the teachers that God has given to His church, whether in person or through their writings, to understand the good and necessary consequences of the Word of God.

None other than the apostle Peter declared that some things in Paul's writings were hard to understand (2 Peter 3:16); the Ethiopian could not understand the scroll of Isaiah unless someone taught him (Acts 8:31); Daniel and Zechariah did not understand several of their visions; and the instances of the disciples' misunderstandings of Jesus Himself are too numerous to cite.

5

Practical Conclusions

The importance of the principle of good and necessary consequence has been largely neglected. It is no accident that we have simultaneously seen widespread criticism of systematic theology as well as the theology of the Westminster Standards. In light of the preceding chapters, a few practical conclusions are in order.

The New Testament Use of the Old Testament

First, in instances similar to those given in chapter 1, the good and necessary consequence principle helps us better to understand the New Testament use of the Old Testament Scriptures. In turn, this provides a potential model as to how we should approach our own use of Scripture.[1] Christ and His apostles expected their deductions from

---

1. One book that is particularly interesting in this regard is D. A. Carson and G. K. Beale, eds., *Commentary on the New Testament Use of the Old Testament* (Grand Rapids: Baker, 2007). The various authors in this volume approach this question from somewhat varying perspectives.

Scripture to be convincing even to an unbelieving audience. Are they less convincing to us? If the New Testament authors cannot serve as a model for our use of the Bible, then what model are we left with? It is true that we must give our primary attention to the exposition of Scripture in its original context, yet the Bible was given by a triune God who knows the consequences of His own words. Moreover, He has given us examples demonstrating that He expects us to recognize and connect these consequences in our study of the Bible. Let us learn from contemporary methods of exegesis, but let our exegesis rest ultimately upon the model provided by the Scriptures themselves.

Perhaps the greatest strength of precritical exegesis (i.e., pre-Enlightenment and pre-historical-critical method) is that it sought to apply the Protestant doctrine of the sufficiency of Scripture to the Bible itself. Are we willing to admit arguments deduced from the general teaching of the Word of God? Have you rejected certain doctrines and practices solely on the grounds that there is no express statement or example given from Scripture to establish them? Let us beware lest Christ's indictment against the Sadducees fall upon us: "Ye do err, not knowing the scriptures" (Matt. 22:29)!

Application in Preaching

Second, good and necessary consequence makes application in preaching both possible and effective. Unless sermon application is legitimately deduced from the statements and doctrines of the text of Scripture, it will fail to have the force of divine authority behind it.[2] The apostle James deduced from the Old Testament example of Elijah's fervent prayer for rain that "the effectual fervent prayer of a righteous man availeth much" (James 5:16–17). All of the apostles likewise rooted their doctrines and applications in inferences drawn from the Old Testament Scriptures. It is only when we utilize this model that our sermon application will bear the force of divine authority behind it. When we preach the text "Believe on the Lord Jesus Christ, and thou shalt be saved, and thy house" (Acts 16:31), our hearers must deduce by good and necessary consequence that if they believe on the Lord Jesus Christ, then they, too—like the prison keeper whom Paul originally addressed—shall be saved. We must press them with such inferences in our preaching. If the condition of obtaining salvation is faith in Jesus Christ, and whoever calls upon the name of the Lord shall be saved (Joel 2:32), then our hearers must call upon the name of the Lord in faith to be saved. Without a simple inference such as this one, personal assurance of salvation would be impossible. The Bible commands us to "give diligence to make your calling and election sure" (2 Peter 1:10), yet it never identifies us, by our names, as the elect. Those who are elect come to Christ, and Christ has promised not to cast out

---

2. The best treatment that I have read concerning how to root sermon application in a proper use of Scripture is John Carrick, *The Imperative of Preaching: A Theology of Sacred Rhetoric* (Edinburgh: Banner of Truth, 2002).

any who come to Him (John 6:37). If we come to Christ, then we were given to Christ. If we come to Christ, then we may be assured that He will keep us and preserve us in faith (v. 39). If we come to Christ with sincere faith, then we may be assured that our names have been written in the Lamb's Book of Life from the foundation of the world, just as truly as if we had read our names in Holy Scripture.[3] This kind of application would be impossible without good and necessary consequence.

Creeds and Confessions

Third, good and necessary consequence is the foundation of creeds and confessions of faith. Without good and necessary consequence, this Explorations in Reformed Confessional Theology series would be fruitless for the church. Doctrinal formulations would be inherently unbiblical without this principle. This is closely related to the earlier assertions that in this principle we find the justification for doing systematic theology. The purpose of a confession of faith, whether of an individual or a church, is not simply to quote what the Bible says, but to explain what the Bible means. Concerning the necessity of creeds and confessions, James Bannerman wrote:

---

3. The Puritan Joseph Alleine (1634–1668) gave the following sound advice concerning election and conversion: "You begin at the wrong end if you first dispute about your election. Prove your conversion, and then never doubt your election." Joseph Alleine, *A Sure Guide to Heaven*, originally published as *An Alarm to the Unconverted, in a Serious Treatise* (1671; repr., Edinburgh: Banner of Truth, 1989), 30.

The language of Scripture is the best language to express God's mind. But it does not follow from this that it is the best language to express my mind, even although I may mean to express to another man, so that there shall be no misunderstanding between us, the very same truths which God has expressed. With the change in the meaning of language which takes place from age to age,—with the different interpretations actually put upon the terms of Scripture by multitudes,—with the various and even opposite senses which reason, or prejudice, or error has made to be associated with its phraseology; the very words of the Bible may not be the best words to declare my mind and belief to another man, so that betwixt him and me there shall be no equivocation, or reservation, or guile.... The Church may take the Bible into its hand, and hold it up to the view of the world as the one profession of its faith; but in doing so it is merely exhibiting the mind of God, not declaring its own.[4]

It is our duty to confess our faith to one another as well as to a lost and dying world. We cannot do this unless we conclude that the Bible actually means something and unless we tell people what we believe it means. Both

---

4. Bannerman, *Church of Christ*, 1:297–98. Note the following comment as well: "Confessions of Faith are not immediately designed to give an account of what the Holy Ghost says concerning such an article, but of what such a person or church believes; and so the words of a Creed or Confession are not expressions of the will of the Holy Ghost, but of our faith, and of the mind of the subscriber." William Dunlop, *The Uses of Creeds and Confessions of Faith*, ed. James Buchanan (Edinburgh: Johnstone, Hunter, and Co., 1857), 141.

heretics and the orthodox can quote the same Scriptures to one another and intend very different results from those texts. Without drawing consequences and conclusions from Scripture, we would be utterly unable to distinguish what we believe from what others believe. Let us then use this principle carefully, holding closely to the Word of God, but let us not neglect it. Whether or not we recognize it, the principle of good and necessary consequence is woven into the very heart of our Christian profession and practice.

Bibliography

Alleine, Joseph. *A Sure Guide to Heaven*. Edinburgh: Banner
of Truth Trust, 1989. First published in 1671 as *An
Alarm to the Unconverted, in a Serious Treatise*.

Bannerman, James. *The Church of Christ: A Treatise on the
Nature, Power, Ordinances, Discipline, and Govern-
ment of the Christian Church*. Edinburgh: T&T
Clark, 1868. Reprint, Birmingham, Ala.: Solid
Ground Christian Books, 2009.

Bavinck, Herman. *Reformed Dogmatics*. Edited by John Bolt.
Translated by John Vriend. 4 vols. Grand Rapids:
Baker, 2004.

Beattie, Francis R. *The Presbyterian Standards: An Exposition
of the Westminster Confession of Faith and Catechisms*.
Richmond, Va.: Southern Presbyterian Press, 1896.

Berkhof, Louis. *Principles of Biblical Interpretation*. Grand
Rapids: Baker, 1950.

Bierma, Lyle D. "Law and Grace in Ursinus' Doctrine of the
Natural Covenant." *Protestant Scholasticism: Essays
in Reassessment*, edited by Carl R. Trueman and
R. Scott Clark, 96–110. Carlisle, UK: Paternoster
Press, 2005.

Bolton, Samuel. *The True Bounds of Christian Freedom, or a Treatise wherein the Rights of the Law Are Vindicated, the Liberties of Grace Maintained, and the Several Late Opinions against the Law Are Examined and Confuted*. London, 1656.

Brakel, Wilhelmus à. *The Christian's Reasonable Service*. Edited by Joel R. Beeke. Translated by Bartel Elshout. Grand Rapids: Reformation Heritage Books, 1992.

Burroughs, Jeremiah. *Gospel Worship*. Edited by Don Kistler. Morgan, Pa.: Soli Deo Gloria Publications, 1990. First published in London, 1648.

Calvin, John. *Institutes of the Christian Religion*. Edited by John T. McNeill. Translated by Ford Lewis Battles. Philadelphia: Westminster Press, 1960.

Carrick, John. *The Imperative of Preaching: A Theology of Sacred Rhetoric*. Edinburgh: Banner of Truth, 2002.

Carson, D. A. and G. K. Beale, eds. *Commentary on the New Testament Use of the Old Testament*. Grand Rapids: Baker, 2007.

Cheynell, Francis. *The Divine Triunity of the Father, Son, and Holy Spirit*. London, 1650.

Collinson, Patrick. "England and International Calvinism, 1558–1640." In *From Cranmer to Sancroft: Essays on English Religion in the Sixteenth and Seventeenth Centuries*, 75–100. New York: Hambledon Continuum, 2006.

Dickson, David. *A Commentary on the Psalms*. Edinburgh: Banner of Truth, 1959. First published in three parts in Edinburgh, 1653–1655.

———. *Truth's Victory over Error: An Exposition of the Westminster Confession of Faith*. Edinburgh: Banner of Truth, 2007.

Dixon, Philip. *Christ's Churches Purely Reformed: A Social History of Calvinism.* New Haven: Yale University Press, 2002.

———. *Nice and Hot Disputes: The Doctrine of the Trinity in the Seventeenth Century.* London: T&T Clark, 2003.

Dunlop, William. *The Uses of Creeds and Confessions of Faith.* Edited by James Buchanan. Edinburgh: Johnstone, Hunter, and Co., 1857.

Durham, James. *Clavis Cantici, or, An Exposition of the Song of Solomon, With an Introduction by John Owen, D. D.* London, 1668.

Fairbairn, Patrick. *Typology of Scripture: Viewed in Conexion with the Entire Scheme of Divine Dispensations, Second Edition Much Enlarged and Improved, Two Volumes in One.* New York: Funk & Wagnalls, 1900; repr., Grand Rapids: Kregel, 1989 .

Fesko, John V. *Water, Word, and Spirit: A Reformed Perspective on Baptism.* Grand Rapids: Reformation Heritage Books, 2010.

Gaffin, Richard B. *Resurrection and Redemption: A Study in Paul's Soteriology.* Phillipsburg, N.J.: P&R, 1987.

———. "The Vitality of Reformed Systematic Theology." In *The Faith Once Delivered: Essays in Honor of Wayne R. Spear,* edited by Anthony T. Selvaggio. Phillipsburg, N.J.: P&R, 2007.

Gillespie, George. *A Treatise of Miscellany Questions: Wherein Many Useful Questions and Cases of Conscience Are Discussed and Resolved; for the Satisfaction of Those, Who Desire Nothing More, Than to Search for and Find Out Precious Truths, in the Controversies of These Times.* University of Edinburgh, 1649.

Heflin, Joel L. "Omnipotent Sweetness? Puritanism Versus Socinianism." *Puritan Reformed Journal* 1, no. 2 (July 2009): 64–95.

Hendriksen, William. *New Testament Commentary: Exposition of the Gospel according to Matthew.* Grand Rapids: Baker, 1973.

Kaiser, Walter and Moises Silva. *An Introduction to Biblical Hermeneutics.* Grand Rapids: Zondervan, 1994.

Kelly, Douglas F. *Systematic Theology.* Vol. 1, *Grounded in Holy Scripture and Understood in Light of the Church: The God Who Is; The Holy Trinity.* Rossshire, UK: Christian Focus, 2008.

Kelly, J. N. D. *Early Christian Doctrines.* New York: HarperCollins, 1960.

Knapp, Henry. "Understanding the Mind of God: John Owen and Seventeenth-Century Exegetical Methodology." PhD diss., Calvin Theological Seminary, 2002.

Kostenberger, Andreas J. *A Theology of John's Gospel and Letters.* Grand Rapids: Zondervan, 2009.

Kostenberger, Andreas J., and Scott R. Swain. *Father, Son, and Spirit: The Trinity and John's Gospel.* Westmont, Ill.: InterVarsity, 2008.

Lee, Brian J. *Johannes Cocceius and the Exegetical Roots of Federal Theology.* Göttingen, Germany: Vandenhoeck and Ruprecht, 2009.

Letham, Robert. *The Holy Trinity: In Scripture, History, Theology, and Worship.* Phillipsburg, N.J.: P&R, 2004.

———. *Union with Christ: In Scripture, History, and Theology.* Phillipsburg, N.J.: P&R Publishing, 2011.

———. *The Westminster Assembly: Reading Its Theology in Historical Context.* Phillipsburg, N.J.: P&R Publishing, 2009.

MacLeod, Donald. *The Person of Christ*. Westmont, Ill.: InterVarsity, 1998.

Marcel, Pierre. *The Biblical Doctrine of Infant Baptism: Sacrament of the Covenant of Grace*. Translated by Philip Edgcumbe Hughes. New York: Westminster Publishing House, 1951. Reprint, 2000.

———. *The Relevance of Preaching*. Edited by William Childs Robinson. Translated by Rob Roy McGregor. Grand Rapids: Baker, 1963.

Matthison, Keith A. *The Shape of Sola Scriptura*. Moscow, Idaho: Canon Press, 2001.

McGraw, Ryan M. "The Consequences of Reformed Worship: The Call to Worship, Baptism, the Offering, and the Benediction in Corporate Worship." ThM thesis, Greenville Presbyterian Theological Seminary, 2008.

———. *The Day of Worship: Reassessing the Christian Life in Light of the Sabbath*. Grand Rapids: Reformation Heritage Books, 2011.

———. "A Pastor's Analysis of Emphases in Preaching: Two False Dichotomies and Three Conclusions." *Puritan Reformed Journal* 2, no. 1 (January 2010): 266–76.

———. "Principles of Sabbath Keeping: Jesus and Westminster." *Puritan Reformed Journal* 3, no. 1 (January 2011): 316–27.

———. "Retaining Scripture in Our Minds and in Our Hearts." *Katechomen: The Online Journal of Greenville Presbyterian Theological Seminary*. http:// katekomen. gpts.edu/2010/04/retaining-scripture -in-our-minds-and-in.html. April 1, 2010.

———. "A Review of Douglas F. Kelly's *Systematic Theology Volume One*." *Westminster Theological Journal* 72, no. 1 (Spring 2010): 193–97.

McKim, Donald K., ed. *Historical Handbook of Biblical Inter-preters*. Westmont, Ill.: InterVarsity, 1998.

Milton, Anthony. "Puritanism and the Continental Reformed Churches." In *The Cambridge Companion to Puritanism*. Edited by John Coffey and Paul C. H. Lim, 109–126. Cambridge: Cambridge University Press, 2008.

Muller, Richard A. *Post-Reformation Reformed Dogmatics*. Vol. 2, *Holy Scripture, The Cognitive Foundation of Theology*. Grand Rapids: Eerdmans, 2003.

Muller, Richard A., and John L. Thompson, eds. *Biblical Interpretation in the Era of Reformation*. Grand Rapids: Eerdmans, 1996.

Muller, Richard A., and Rowland S. Ward. *Scripture and Worship: Biblical Interpretation and the Directory for Worship*. Phillipsburg, N.J.: P&R, 2007.

Murray, John. "The Unity of the Old and New Testaments." In *The Collected Writings of John Murray*, 23–26. Edinburgh: Banner of Truth, 1976.

Nolland, John. *The Gospel of Matthew: A Commentary on the Greek Text*. Grand Rapids: Eerdmans, 2005.

Oberman, Heiko A. *The Harvest of Medieval Theology: Gabriel Biel and Late Medieval Nominalism*. Grand Rapids: Baker, 2000.

Packer, J. I. "Is Systematic Theology a Mirage? An Introductory Discussion." In *Doing Theology in Today's World: Essays in Honor of Kenneth S. Kantzer*. Edited by John D. Woodbridge and Thomas Edward McKomisky. Grand Rapids: Zondervan, 1991.

Prestwick, Menna, ed. *International Calvinism, 1541–1715*. Oxford: Clarendon Press, 1985.

Robertson, O. Palmer. *Prophet of the Coming Day of the Lord: The Message of Joel.* Durham, UK: Evangelical Press, 1995.

Schaff, Philip. "Canones et Decreta Dogmatica Concilii Tridentini." In vol. 2 of *The Creeds of Christendom: With a History and Critical Notes*, 77–206. Grand Rapids: Baker, 1998. First published in New York by Harper & Row, 1931.

Shedd, W. G. T. Introduction to *Augustine on the Trinity*. In *Nicene and Post-Nicene Fathers*, edited by Philip Schaff. 1st series, vol. 3, 1887. Reprint, Peabody, Mass: Hendrickson Publishers, 2004.

Steinmetz, David C. "The Superiority of Precritical Exegesis." In *A Guide to Contemporary Hermeneutics: Major Trends in Biblical Interpretation*, edited by Donald K. McKim, 65–77. Grand Rapids: Eerdmans, 1986.

Thiselton, Anthony C. *The First Epistle to the Corinthians, New International Greek Testament Commentary.* Grand Rapids: Eerdmans, 2000.

Thomas Aquinas. *Summa Theologica.* 1274. http://www.corpusthomisticum.org/sth1001.html.

Toon, Peter. *Our Triune God: A Biblical Portrayal of the Trinity.* Vancouver: Regent College, 1996.

Trueman, Carl. R. *John Owen: Reformed Catholic, Renaissance Man.* Burlington, Vt.: Ashgate, 2007.

Turretin, Francis. *Institutes of Elenctic Theology.* Edited by James Dennison Jr. Translated by George Musgrave Giger. 1696. Reprint, Phillipsburg, N.J.: P&R, 1992.

Van Asselt, Willem, and Eef Dekker, eds. *Reformation and Scholasticism: An Ecumenical Enterprise.* Grand Rapids: Baker, 2001.

Waldron, Samuel E. *A Modern Exposition of the 1689 Baptist Confession of Faith*. Webster, N.Y.: Evangelical Press, 2005.

Warfield, Benjamin Breckinridge. "The Right of Systematic Theology." In *Selected Shorter Writings of Benjamin B. Warfield*, edited by John E. Meeter, 219–79. Phillipsburg, N.J.: P&R, 1970.

————. "The Westminster Doctrine of Holy Scripture." In *The Works of B. B. Warfield*. New York: Oxford University Press, 1932. Reprint, Grand Rapids: Baker, 2003.

Weir, David A. *The Origins of Federal Theology in Sixteenth Century Reformation Thought*. Oxford: Clarendon Press, 1990.

Westcott, B. F. *The Epistle to the Hebrews: The Greek Text with Notes and Essays*. 1892. Reprint, Grand Rapids: Eerdmans, 1977.

Whitaker, William. *Disputations on Holy Scripture*. Translated by William Fitzgerald. London, 1588. Reprint, Orlando: Soli Deo Gloria, 2005.

Williams, C. J. "Good and Necessary Consequence in the Westminster Confession." In *The Faith Once Delivered: Essays in Honor of Wayne R. Spear*, edited by Anthony T. Selvaggio, 171–90. Phillipsburg, N.J.: P&R, 2007.

Scripture Index